CW00642775

THE COMPLETE VISITOR'S GUIDE TO LOCH NESS, INVERNESS AND THE LOCH NESS MONSTER

The Complete Visitor's Guide

to
Loch Ness, Inverness
and the
Loch Ness
Monster

Andy Owens

MAINSTREAM
PUBLISHING
EDINBURGH AND LONDON

As always, with love,
to Mom (Dorothy Owens), Dad (Jack
Owens), to David Owens and
Silvia Haller.

Also for Chris and Julie Ellis, Jodie,
Connor and Brandon.

Copyright © Andy Owens, 2000

First published in Great Britain in 2000 by
MAINSTREAM PUBLISHING COMPANY (EDINBURGH) LTD
7 Albany Street
Edinburgh EH1 3UG

ISBN 1 84018 307 1

Cover photograph © Steve Feltham
Inverness street map reproduced from Inverness Street Plan by R.P.A. Smith
Loch Ness map © Wendy Price

A catalogue record for this book is available from the British Library

Typeset in Garamond and Gill Sans
Printed and bound in Finland by WS Bookwell

ACKNOWLEDGEMENTS

Many thanks to Colin A. Simpson, Inverness area manager, and staff of the Highlands of Scotland Tourist Board, and the residents of Inverness and Loch Ness for their kindness and help over the years; licensees, staff and customers of the Dores Inn; Lynne Illingworth of the *Inverness Courier*; the people of Fort Augustus, particularly Mr Murdo McKay of the post office, staff of A. & W.J. Newsagents and staff of the Scots Kitchen; Commander A.G.W. (Bill) Bellars OBE of Kent; Mrs Wendy Dinsdale; Mr Richard Carter; Mr George Edwards; Mr R.P.A. Smith and Mrs Wendy Price for reproduction of maps and Chris Fitch and Shirley Kavanagh of Ordnance Survey. Particular thanks to book publishers and magazines for allowing me to quote from their works, including: Hamish Hamilton Ltd; Terence Dalton Ltd; Visible Ink Press, Detroit, for their book *Unexplained* by Jerome Clark; Suzanne Greig of *The Scotsman*; many thanks for research material from Elaine Hart of *Illustrated London News*; Zoe Wales and Helen Slane of *New Scientist*; Dr David Munro of the Royal Scottish Geographical Society and the Clan Munro; thanks to Dr P.J.H. Lambshead of the British Natural History Museum, Andy Horton of the British Marine Life Study Society, and Dr Roger Jones of Lancaster University for answering my questions. Also those people I didn't meet, though whose work greatly interested me: Dr Robert H. Rines (Academy of Applied Sciences, Massachusetts); Prof. Roy P. Mackal (the University of Chicago); Nicholas Witchell; Dr Denys W. Tucker; the late Charles Weikoff, and all the people mentioned in this book, including Alistair Boyd and David Martin for their book *Nessie: The Surgeon's Photograph Exposed*. Best wishes to Tom Perrott, Ricky Burgess, Matthew Hutton, Jim

Davis, Paul Morgan, Steve Wyatt, Craig Horswood and family, Steve Bentley, Sarah Colquitt and Steve Peckover. All the best to Steve and Julie, Dave and Ruth, Rick and Michelle, Paul and Charlotte, Fowler, Debbie, Julie, Chantelle, Hayley, Chris Bray and all at Inn-Cognito Restaurant, Halifax.

A big thank you to Siân Braes, Bill Campbell, Sarah Edwards, Elaine Scott and all at Mainstream for turning this book into a reality.

Special thanks for taking time to answer my questions and proof-read my work detailing their research to Steve Feltham, 'Rip' Hepple and Adrian Shine.

Finally, thanks to the late Tim Dinsdale, whom I never had the pleasure of meeting, but whose book *Loch Ness Monster* hooked the interest of a certain teenager – and never quite let go.

CONTENTS

To Beau

To Cannich
and Glen Affric **A831**

Drumnadrochit
Lewiston

Meall Fuar
Mhonaidh
696

*Loch
nam Breac
Dearga*

Balbeg

A82

Loch

Creag nan Eun
413m

A887

River Moriston

Invermoriston

To Kyle
of Lochalsh

Carn nan
Dubh Lochan
594m

Beinn
a' Bhacaidh
552m

*Loch
Knockie*

Knockie
Lodge

W

*Loch
Tarff*

B862

Fort Augustus

River Oich

A82

To Corrieyairack Pass

To Fort William

© Wendy Price
Cartographic Services

INTRODUCTION

The idea for this book came to me in August 1998. I had been visiting the area every year since 1995 because of a serious interest in the Loch Ness Monster mystery. On my visits I found that even after you had stripped away the tourism, fake photos and media sensationalism, there still remained a considerable hard core of evidence – from close-range, multi-witness sightings to unexplained sonar contacts – for large, unknown animals in Loch Ness.

Having looked for a guidebook to the area I was surprised that there wasn't one. Surprising since Loch Ness gets half a million tourists every year – Inverness considerably more.

I did receive some criticism due to the fact that I'm a visitor rather than local expert – but I still maintain that it takes a visitor to write a visitor's guidebook, and this I have done, but with much help from local people and experts and, particularly, the Highlands of Scotland Tourist Board.

As well as information on accommodation to suit all pockets and tastes and the recommendation of restaurants, inns and tourist attractions, I have included other information which visitors really need to know: petrol filling stations and in-house shops, some of which are open all night; supermarkets for those on a self-catering holiday, perhaps touring the area for a little longer; banks and building societies and availability of cash dispensers; hairdressers, clothes shops, chemists, opticians, baby goods hire, department stores, fish and chip shops, pizza delivery; taxi services and car breakdown and recovery. The grid references given refer to the Inverness street map.

This guide reflects my interest in the area which, although initially sparked off by the Loch Ness mystery, has since expanded into the wealth of attractions – historic, prehistoric and the modern culture – of both Inverness and Loch Ness.

Like me, you will no doubt find that 'Highland Hospitality' is not just some clever advertising catchphrase, but one that is sincere and accurate – and local people, on the whole, are kind, courteous, helpful and welcoming, which may very well bring you back to the area, or to another part of Scotland, time and time again.

The first part of this guide concerns the mystery itself and, while I have drawn on the many books, articles and TV documentaries concerning the subject, this isn't simply a rehash or a mixture of fact and fantasy. I have interviewed two of the modern Nessie researchers – leader of the Loch Ness Project Adrian Shine and independent researcher Steve Feltham – and added my own view of the mystery. All I can do, however, is present the cases for and against and, ultimately, it is up to you to make up your own mind.

PART 1: THE HISTORY OF A MYSTERY

LOOKING FOR LOCH NESS MONSTERS

'I often wonder why it is that any explanation of the phenomenon in Loch Ness, however complicated and farfetched it may be, is more acceptable than the obvious one, namely, that the loch is the home of an uncommon animal.'

(Letter to *The Scotsman* from
C.E.W., 24 March 1954)

Gaze out across the vast expanse of Loch Ness and you will begin to appreciate why it has gained a reputation as the home of monsters. In fact, stare into the peat-stained waters for long enough and you may convince yourself you can see black shapes which appear to dart back and forth just below the surface.

The mystery first hit the headlines in 1933, when Mr and Mrs George Spicer described how a large grey animal with an undulating neck hurried across the road in front of their car. The very next year brought another major sighting from Mr and Mrs John Mackay – and the infamous surgeon's photograph.

At this time a new road had been completed along the loch's northern shore and miles of foliage cleared away to give motorists an uninterrupted view of the loch. From then on, the sightings came in thick and fast and are still being reported to this day.

It has recently been proven that Nessie cannot be a long-necked plesiosaur, which was the image that captured the world's imagination. However, the view that Nessie can't exist purely because it cannot be a plesiosaur is a nonsensical argument.

Scientific research at Loch Ness has helped, not

hindered, the monster quest. Studies of the food supply or the geology or the biology of this beautiful lake have helped to dispel many myths about Nessie – to separate fact from fantasy – for this is where realists and romanticists part company.

What follows is a brief history, and update, on the Loch Ness mystery. While theories have been dashed, and sightings and photos denounced as fakes and mistakes, I hope to show that there still remains a sizeable chunk of mystery to be solved; still a case to answer at Loch Ness, Scotland.

THE CLASSIC SIGHTINGS

It has been said that extraordinary claims require extraordinary proof and nowhere is this more appropriate than at Loch Ness – as conclusive evidence remains teasingly absent. Sightings that sceptics can't dismiss as curious waves and boat wakes, mirages, wildlife, driftwood and odd tricks of the light, are those which they prefer to sweep under the proverbial rug. Those eye-witness accounts, dubbed 'classic' cases, such as close-range, multi-witness and land sightings, or a combination of these, flatly refuse to be explained away; in fact, some of these sightings will never go away. Pushed into a corner, sceptics will often go for the jugular and explain that all of these people are lying.

People like Margaret Cameron and her brother and sister who, just prior to the First World War, 'fled in terror' after watching a 20-foot animal, 'like a huge caterpillar', crash through foliage on the other side of tiny Inchnacardoch Bay.

Or Brother Richard Horan, one of the Benedictine monks at Fort Augustus Abbey. On 28 May 1934, while working in the Abbey's boathouse, he spent five minutes watching a long-necked animal dart about in the water at a distance of just 30 yards, before it dived. Three other people corroborated his sighting. Some years later, his colleague, Father Gregory Brusey, and a friend, Roger Pugh, organist at St James's Cathedral, watched a 'terrible commotion' in the waters of the bay. This was followed by the appearance of a ten-foot head and neck which broke the surface, travelled towards them for nearly twenty seconds, then sank out of sight.

In 1963, farmers Hugh and Jim Ayton, and three friends, watched a long neck and two humps 'which belonged to what was obviously one large animal', then four of them followed it down the loch in a motor boat until it submerged.

In August 1952, Greta Finlay and her 12-year-old son, Harry, a keen angler, saw a 15-foot, long-necked animal looking at them from a distance of 20 yards which 'paralysed them with fear'. The young boy was so frightened he never went fishing again.

And the list goes on.

SCIENTIFIC DOGMA

By 1960 the press had been inundated with hundreds of reports of eyewitness sightings, and there seemed a need for a proper investigative body, though it would still take two years to form the first of such groups.

Although the pastime of 'monster-hunting' would gain semi-credibility in later years as 'crypto-zoology' (the study of 'cryptids' or unknown animals), the scientific community preferred to avoid an affiliation with such a fringe subject.

Loch Ness researcher Alistair Boyd says, 'The stability of their careers probably depends, to some extent, on maintaining the status quo. Nobody really wants to stick their neck out, as it were, and go looking for something which could prove to be an embarrassment in their careers.'

Dr P.J.H. Lambshead, a biologist at the Natural History Museum, has been quoted as saying that scientists always gave a nervous twitch whenever the loch was mentioned. 'As you can quite imagine, it could be the kiss of death to your career,' he says. 'One of my predecessors was actually sacked from his job for going up on the loch.' That man was Dr Denys W. Tucker, principal scientific officer at the Museum, who had planned an expedition to the loch for 27 June 1960, though the team arrived without him.

But why was Dr Tucker so convinced that the loch held some unsolved mystery? Well, he didn't just 'believe' in it – he knew there was something to be proven. Exactly four months later he published a letter in the highly respected *New Scientist* magazine, which included the words: 'I, a professional marine zoologist of respectable experience, did see a large hump travelling across flat, calm water between Inchnacardoch Bay and Glendoe on 22 March 1959, and do quite unashamedly assert that it belonged to an unknown animal.'

MONSTER WATCH

From the very first nationally reported sighting to those in recent years, the noted absence of the British scientific establishment from the shores of Loch Ness left the mystery to be solved by enthusiastic amateurs and transatlantic scientists. One such 'amateur' was aeronautical engineer Tim Dinsdale, who arrived at the loch in 1960 and embarked on countless expeditions throughout the rest of his life, until his sudden death in 1987. In April of 1960, he took what is widely regarded as the best moving footage of the monster. It seems to show a featureless black hump moving away from Dinsdale's camera, from his position on a hillside overlooking Foyers Bay. The film was consequently shown on the BBC TV programme *Panorama*, followed by a studio debate on the subject. More than any other factor, this film was instrumental in bringing forward plans for a research group.

In May 1962, the LNPIB (Loch Ness Phenomena Investigation Bureau Ltd) was founded by David James MP, Constance Whyte, and naturalists Richard Fitter and Sir Peter Scott. During its ten-year existence, complete with 50 volunteers manning long-range surveillance cameras, their efforts went largely unrewarded. Several lengths of footage were taken – most notably by Dick Raynor and Les Durkin – though the objects were too far away to ascertain conclusive identification. By the time the LNPIB folded in 1972, it was clear that a change of approach was needed. If Nessie would not come to the camera, then the cameras would have to go underwater. The Monster Watch was set to become a Monster Hunt.

MONSTER HUNT

In regard to the mystery, and the scepticism of scientists, co-director of the LNPIB and author Constance Whyte had the following to say in her book *More Than A Legend*: 'There is a challenge to British scientists on their own doorstep and if it is not taken up, the initiative may pass to others – a team of wealthy enthusiasts may arrive from across the sea to solve the problem for us.'

Ms Whyte's sentiment turned out to be more prophetic than perhaps she could ever have anticipated. The very next year brought one such 'wealthy enthusiast from across the sea' and, in many years to come, he and his dedicated research team would play a major part in the investigation on successive expeditions to the loch.

This enthusiast arrived in the form of Dr Bob Rines who, on a chance visit to the loch in 1958, heard about the mystery and became intrigued. As Constance Whyte had warned, whilst the British establishment as a whole was unwilling, indeed stoutly refusing, even to consider that there may be any 'mystery' to the loch, their American counterparts were taking the initiative, beginning sonar expeditions in the 1970s.

However, it was not as if the British monster-hunting fraternity resented the transatlantic interest at Loch Ness. On the contrary. The American research teams were not only to offer much-needed technical expertise and equipment, not to mention financial support to the flagging LNPIB, with whom they worked alongside, but also took the time and patience to listen to accounts from eyewitnesses who had previously been ignored and even ridiculed.

Dr Bob Rines has been described by various people who have worked with him as the nearest real-life version of the American Dream. A respected patent lawyer and founder of a law school, he quickly made his name in that field, before moving on to greener pastures. He trained as a scientist and engineer, assisted in the development of both radar and sonar, wrote stage musicals, and was awarded an honorary degree. As he became more intrigued by the mystery, Dr Rines's trips to the loch became more frequent. However, his hunch turned to total conviction on the evening of 23 June 1971, when he and his wife Carol, and friends Wing Commander Basil and Mrs Freddie Cary, watched a long, greyish hump appear in Urquhart Bay. They estimated its size to be around 20 feet long, having compared it to a fishing boat anchored nearby, as it moved around the surface, against the wind currents, and then sank. Rines concluded, 'This has finally destroyed any last doubts I had that what we are dealing with is a very large creature here at Loch Ness.'

He returned the very next year, accompanied by fellow scientists from his Academy of Applied Sciences, of Boston, Massachusetts. Armed with an electronic stroboscopic camera, they recorded what is regarded by many as the best – albeit most controversial – evidence to date. The LNPIB had just disbanded and several of its now former members were present at 1.45 a.m. on 8 August 1972. Three were sat in the observation boat moored in Urquhart Bay, watching a mass of tiny dots on the sonar chart, indicating a shoal of salmon. Then, suddenly, the dots turned to dashes, as if the fish were rapidly moving away from the area, before a larger trace appeared on the sonar chart – a big, heavy, black trace which appeared to be chasing the fish. Initially the team thought it showed two or three fish moving together, but it continued to grow in size and density. Before long, the sonar trace ceased; the boat had begun to drift around in the water and the contact was lost – but the team were very excited about what they would find on camera. They studied thousands of frames of film which showed nothing but the murky waters of the loch. However, the team found three frames which appeared to show an object reflecting the strobe light back at the camera. When computer enhanced, one of the frames seems to show a diamond-shaped flipper just in front of the camera.

The next successful Rines expedition in 1975 achieved two more photographs, one which greatly resembled the plesiosaur, as if posing in a full-body shot, and another photo of what was described as a 'hideous, gargoyle-like head with protruding horns and a gaping mouth'.

The three images remain largely controversial even to this day, with claims that they had been 'touched up' by magazine editors to make them appear more convincing. Sceptics and believers are as divided as ever.

THE CLASSIC PHOTOGRAPHS

Researchers have been fairly scathing of Nessie pics – and not without good reason. There is no getting over the fact that most, if not all, of them are fakes – or mistakes. Polythene bags, bales of hay covered with tarpaulin, oil drums and other inanimate objects have all been used to dupe the public. And, it has to be said, these have proved more damaging to the real mystery than any other single factor, since it is now largely viewed as little more than tourist attraction and silly-season joke.

When big-game hunter M.A. Wetherell and cameraman Gustave Pauli were hired by a national newspaper to find Nessie, in 1934, their expedition was discredited after fake 'monster' footprints were found on the shore. In *More Than A Legend*, Constance Whyte refers to them, fairly or not, as Mr Pilt and Mr Down, after the infamous archaeological hoax. It is claimed that Wetherell, angry at being discredited, set about faking a photo and asked Colonel Robert Kenneth Wilson, a respected gynaecologist, to act as frontsman for what came to be known as 'The Surgeon's Photograph'.

In 1994, two members of the Loch Ness and Morar Scientific Project, zoologist David Martin and Loch Ness researcher Alistair Boyd, interviewed model maker Christian Spurling, who gave a death-bed confession claiming that he had helped Wetherell to fake the photo, which sparked off a major controversy. American journalist Richard Smith attempted to recreate the photo by using two models to see which one matched the original image.

Smith believes the photo could show the four-foot head and neck of a real animal shot from a distance, while Boyd and Martin claimed it was a one-foot model head, fixed to a toy submarine, and shot from a few yards away. (See Further Reading for Martin and Boyd's book detailing their in-depth investigation.)

Interviewed by Esther Rantzen in 1999, independent researcher Steve Feltham said he was amazed that everyone had accepted Spurling's testimony without question. 'No,' said Steve, 'I don't accept such damning testimony as readily. But Spurling is dead now, and the Surgeon's Photograph can no longer be considered as evidence for the existence of the Loch Ness monster.'

One of the reasons that Alistair Boyd was sceptical of the photograph, even from the outset, was due to his own sighting. Parked in a lay-by in 1979 overlooking Urquhart Bay, he and his wife saw 'what was obviously a large, powerful animal turning round just below the surface, then a large dark hump came out of the water. It rolled forward, very much like a whale, we could see the water coming off its back. Neither of us saw it submerge, because we turned round to look for the camera, but by the time we'd turned back again, the water was totally flat calm . . . not a ripple.'

ONE MAN'S QUEST
It has been said that the monster story is so powerful it can change a person's life forever.

When asked to comment on his sighting, Alistair Boyd said, 'It was the most amazing thing I've ever seen in my life. And if I could afford to spend the rest of my life up here looking for another glimpse of it – I would.'

And one man has done just that.

On a family holiday to the loch in 1972, a seven-year-old boy was awed by the sight of a determined group of grown-ups, armed with cameras and a host of other electronic equipment, who had arrived at the lochside to find a 'monster'. His parents bought him a booklet about the mystery to keep him and his brother quiet on the long journey home – and from that day on the lad was hooked. That young boy was Steve Feltham who, fifteen years later, returned to spend three weeks at the lochside – and further trips followed. In fact, it reached the point where Steve resented having to return to his home in Dorset. He would have preferred to stay and live at the loch permanently.

Back at home, business had not been going too well. Steve fondly remembers spending his early years working variously as a potter, graphic artist and bookbinder. However, when money became desperate, he was forced to look to other means to earn a living. He set up in business with his father installing burglar alarms and, from that point onwards, creativity went straight out of the window and he found himself just one more member of the rat race, rushing to the office every day, struggling to pay a mortgage – and he hated it. Speaking to elderly clients, he was constantly reminded that time was swiftly passing by. He knew he was going to regret it if he reached the age of 70 without having done the thing he truly wanted to do, which was to move to the loch full time. So he sold his share in the business, left his girlfriend ('She thought I was crazy. We'd been together a long time and it was coming to an end – she's married now.') and put his house on the market.

This may sound like a rash thing to do, yet how many of us can honestly say we have never dreamed of doing something similar? Steve worked out how it could best be achieved, thus turning the pipe dream into a reality.

The next step was to find a new home – on wheels. He bought an old mobile library from Dorset County Council and, when the house was finally sold, he set off for a new life, finally reaching the shores of Loch Ness in May 1991 – he has never looked back. Steve kept a video diary, which was later to be shown in the BBC TV *Video Diaries* series, and has been approached by numerous journalists, interviewed for documentaries, and appeared on chat shows hosted by Esther Rantzen, John Stapleton and comedian Frank Skinner.

Each time someone meets him they say how unnerved they are by how 'normal' he is – no wild-eyed theories or nervous twitches. Steve Feltham has a healthy respect for his subject. The backbone of his belief was not based on personal experience, but on the hundreds of people who have quietly told him what they have witnessed. Collecting the evidence of others is part of his self-appointed task – and it is convincing. He says, 'The Highlanders are an insular lot, reluctant to talk to outsiders about the mystery for fear of the ridicule that this subject has always attracted. The locals are not in the least bit bothered that many people down south don't believe a word of it. I have sat with old boys of 80 who, once they realise I am not here to take the mick, but have a sincere fascination for the subject and a love of the Highland way of life, quietly tell me of the things they have seen and the things their grandfathers have talked about. I have spoken to a hundred or more of them and I find it impossible – if not arrogant – to call them liars.'

Apart from amassing evidence, the other part of his self-appointed job is to scan the loch's surface with his binoculars with both a stills and video camera on standby. Visitors often ask Steve if he ever gets bored, and his reply is always the same. He never gets bored. His new lifestyle is everything that his old lifestyle wasn't, so when he gave it up he didn't feel like he was sacrificing anything. The magazine *Country Living* asked him to write an article about it. 'Describe a typical day,' they said, but Steve found it impossible as no two days have ever been the same for him. He can only guess what will happen – and it is very rare for that guess to be accurate.

'That is the beauty of what I do,' says Steve, 'the total unpredictability of my day-to-day life. What the day will hold is governed by so many different factors. Like, for example, where I am when I wake up.' Steve made the decision not to settle in any one spot. He regularly moves between four of the lochside villages but spends most of his time parked on the shingle beach at Dores. 'If I ever decided to buy some land I feel sure it would be at Dores, though I don't have any immediate plans to move back into a conventional home just yet.'

When the money from the house was gone, he began to eke out a living making and selling clay model monsters – or 'nessie-serries' – and he only needs to sell two or three a day. 'They certainly keep me ticking over, keep me in food and diesel, which is the reason I make them – to support my full-time hunt.' He survives entirely on his pottery skills and donations from visitors. 'I never know who is going to walk round the side of my van next – or from what corner of the world they're from.' Most are tourists, some are monster-hunters, though he rarely keeps in touch with the various clubs and societies dedicated to the subject, and politely refuses the many invitations to join their ranks. Steve considers them rather odd, remarking it is wonderful to observe the politics and rivalries between the groups who arrive with their grand schemes to solve the mystery – only to leave after a single winter.

Steve spends his days scanning the loch surface from the beach in summer, from the van in winter. His needs are few. The windmill on the roof of the van generates enough power for his light and radio; warmth comes from an old coal-burning stove, and endless stir-fries prepared on a wok to ensure a nutritious and healthy diet. In the summer he bathes in the loch itself, in the winter he heats water and bathes inside, and uses the toilet of the Dores Inn, barely a hundred yards from his home.

First thing in the morning the generator on the roof tells him what conditions on the loch are likely to be. Many sightings have been in the early hours and, while this is an ideal time for monster-hunting, he says, 'With the wind generator buzzing and the wind tapping on my roof, there's no way that I'm getting out of my bed just yet! On calm days the first thing I do is set up my video camera and tripod on the beach. I enjoy nothing more than breakfasting on the shore on a crisp, sunny, Highland morning, watching the water, listening to the radio and drinking coffee. This is just about the only time of day I can rely on having no visitors. So I make a few models, which I may be able to sell later in the day, and keep an eye on the loch while I work.'

Recently, he has been appointed an auxiliary coastguard, now that he possesses a 15-foot dinghy and a mobile phone which a friend in the village recharges for him. He has mentioned plans to buy a boat and echo-sounding equipment and take the search to the water. As it is, he knows that his style of hunting, 'surface watching', will probably never obtain that conclusive piece of footage. 'The best I can hope for, at the present time, is the animal's back cutting through the water – or the glimpse of a head and neck.' However, even footage taken from a fair distance, if it is good enough, could earn him a fortune. This is exactly what happened to Tim Dinsdale.

During my research I was advised that the *Inverness Courier* would be the best place to contact for details of recent sightings because since the demise of the LNPIB in 1972 there exists no active presence on the loch that is specifically directed at collating sightings and investigating the mystery. However, Steve Feltham is one such source. He is to be congratulated on his valuable work, amassing eyewitness accounts, persuading people to fill out report forms and chasing them up. Some of them he sends to Rip Hepple, editor and publisher of *Nessletter* (a newsletter for Nessie researchers), who subsequently prints them, inviting and offering explanations as to the reality of what has been observed. There are some very convincing sightings made by local people, who surely know the difference between otters, seals and larger animals.

Steve agrees with most researchers that the majority of sightings are boat wakes, including a video he has shown taken by an excited tourist who thought he'd snapped a row of humps in the water. 'There is the odd occasion when you think you see something and the adrenaline starts to rush. Then the binoculars reveal the truth.' During his first two months at the loch, Steve kept seeing things out of the corner of his eye, but now claims he can recognise a duck or a chunk of driftwood a mile off. However, there have been exceptions. Video footage which he took himself, and which has been shown on TV, shows what appears to be a head and neck. However, as it moves closer, driven by the tide to the shore, Steve zooms in on it and we can see it for what it really is: a stick upended in the water, trapped in unseen debris beneath the surface!

The question remains, however: why persist in the research when the subject is constantly ridiculed in the media, when concrete evidence remains elusive and some of the best photographs denounced as fakes? Well, apart from many close-range sightings of large creatures in the loch, related to him by the locals – many of whom neither seek nor need publicity and in fact prefer to remain anonymous – he has had one rather odd sighting himself.

'One time, a few years ago, I saw something from the shore at Fort Augustus; a disturbance in the water which couldn't have been made by anything I could explain – but it was gone before I could film it. It was moving against the waves, much as if a jet-ski was going through them, putting up a wash. Because it was at least half a mile away across the bay, neither me nor this lass who was with me could see what the solid object was, but it was something substantial. There wasn't a simple explanation. It lasted only for maybe ten seconds – just enough time to say "What the hell's that?" and watch in amazement.'

He has collected many details of local sightings from the Dores area (incidents which occurred both before and after he arrived there) and one dates from 1983, reported by members of the Inverness Fire Brigade. They had arrived one evening to extinguish a small fire on the beach, when several members saw what looked like a large black hump. Although they could not give it their full attention, they saw it continually submerging and resurfacing before it eventually sank. This possibly supports the theory that the Loch Ness animals are mainly nocturnal creatures, and are attracted by bright lights such as fires. There are similar reports of this nature, including some sightings by members of the LNPIB, who used to shine old wartime spotlights across the surface of the loch at night to test the theory.

Ten years later, Steve interviewed a local man with a similar tale to tell. On 10 August 1993, Roland O'Brian spent ten minutes watching a humped back in Dores Bay. The object caused much splashing, continually halting, turning and moving off again, submerging and reappearing, looking and behaving exactly as a large animal would look and behave if it was hunting fish. Mr O'Brian said he had seen something twice before but 'never anything like this'. He said, 'Any talk of logs, dogs, cattle or deer swimming is nonsense. What I saw was large and capable of going from standstill to extremely fast in seconds.'

Sightings of the 'upturned boat' shape cutting through the water are the most regularly reported descriptions, and certainly the most common seen in Dores Bay. Steve Feltham wonders if the reason for so many sightings here is the presence of fish cages in the waters just off Dores. Because of the feed which has been put into the cages, there are a lot of wild fish in the area eating the surplus that falls through the cage bottoms. Steve asks if it is merely coincidence that bigger creatures are being seen in the area.

On the TV programme *Esther*, Steve described typical Nessie sightings to Esther Rantzen: 'Picture it: it's a calm day and these big animals are swimming about feeding on the fish. There they are, coursing through the water, the roof of their world is silent, and their backs accidentally break the surface, because that top layer of fish in the loch is that close to the surface. So that's the sighting you get. You see this back shooting through the water – you might even see a few fish jumping out the way of it [this has been reported by witnesses] then it's gone, down and away.'

But what will happen if someone else achieves that conclusive piece of Nessie footage? 'Oh, I don't know,' says Steve. 'It's all so unpredictable. That's where the real adventure lies in all this.'

At the end of his *Video Diary* programme Steve explained, 'This programme is not about chasing monsters. It's about realising your own dream – before it's too late.'

And to Steve Feltham that is an end in itself.

A NEW PERSPECTIVE

As the earlier sonar searches were drawing to a close, it seemed clear that a new approach was required; a new perspective on the mystery. British scientists needed to be coaxed to the loch to solve the riddle – but how could this be achieved?

The answer arrived at Loch Ness in the '70s and, since then, no one has spent more time studying Nessie than Adrian Shine. He became so intrigued by the mystery that he gave up his position with a London printing business to come and live by the lochside. He says, 'I thought that here was a great wildlife mystery on my back doorstep – a soft option – and that I could solve it and go home. I've been here 20 years now.'

Adrian Shine is not an academic – and proud of it. A self-taught naturalist, he does not specialise in any one discipline; his interest spans a wide range of subjects from biology to sonar observation, and this has found favour with many scientists who respect his word and judgement. When the LNPIB folded in 1972, Adrian founded the Loch Ness Project, currently based at Drumnadrochit. Today, his interest lies in attracting scientists to the loch to help uncover the many secrets which he believes remain untapped.

He says, 'I want to strip Loch Ness bare, layer by layer, and in finding answers to many seemingly "mundane" scientific puzzles, I hope to find an answer to the one which fascinates the world.'

The years 1973 to 1978 were mainly concentrated on searching the comparatively clear waters of Loch Morar, where 'monster' sightings have also been logged down the years, before he turned his attention to the gloomy depths of Loch Ness. Having bombarded him with questions, he methodically worked his way through them with an ease which, frankly, staggered me. This ease comes from over two decades of research at Britain's number one 'mystery' site, attracting more visitors than Stonehenge and other popular attractions put together. In fact, documentary makers always make a beeline for Adrian Shine. He's the only researcher to have appeared on *The Secrets of Loch Ness, Return to Loch Ness* and zoologist Chris Packham's BBC TV series *The X Creatures*. And this is clearly because of his down-to-earth approach.

The history of the mystery reads like a detective story

and, like a sleuth, Adrian Shine sifts through the evidence. There are many red herrings. Fake photos, ambiguous sonar contacts, video/cine footage showing nothing more than wildlife, debris and standing waves, either seen from a distance or perceived from an odd angle, which are then misinterpreted by the over-imaginative. He says that the majority of sightings, described as 'huge humps', are nothing more than boat wakes, which can still be seen up to half an hour after the boat has passed out of sight. Like any responsible researcher he prefers to consider all possible explanations to account for sightings: curious waves and boat wakes, wildlife, driftwood, mirages – or perhaps just a trick of the light – before considering something a little more unusual. 'Anything you don't understand on the surface of Loch Ness is your "Nessie" – and these people are all seeing their Nessies.'

Spoil-sports they may be, but sceptics, or at least critics, are highly valued at Loch Ness, not least because eyewitnesses are often strangers to the loch and unfamiliar with its changing moods. Former member of the LNPIB Bill Bellars OBE, an ex-anti-submarine specialist, told me that the Bureau used to dismiss about nine out of every ten sightings reported to them.

Tim Dinsdale wasted 20 feet of film on a swirl of waves around a hidden shoal of rocks – two days before taking his famous film. Dr Maurice Burton saw 'three humps' in the same place, at the delta of the River Foyers, which were really three men sat in a dinghy. Rip Hepple witnessed and photographed many examples of 'humps' cutting through the water which have turned out to be no more than just standing waves and boat wakes. William Owen thought he was watching a row of humps for quite some time, before realising they were three ducks flying in tight formation close to the surface. Eric Beckjord thought the objects he filmed, in August 1983, were 'three plesiosaurs in Urquhart Bay', only later accepting they were nothing but ducks.

While Adrian Shine would genuinely like to find an explanation for the mass of eyewitness sightings and sonar contacts, he remains very sceptical of 'head-and-neck' sightings. He points out that although there were many reports of 'monsters' in and around Loch Ness before it became a worldwide media sensation in 1933, there are no pre-1930s reports of a long-necked Nessie.

He puts the famous image down to dinosaur fever, which had gripped the nation after fossilised discoveries at Lyme Regis in the 1840s, exciting those who thought there might be a live specimen living at Loch Ness. Adrian published an article in the now-defunct magazine *The Unexplained* entitled 'A Very Strange Fish?' In it, he stated that Nessie must be a fish – not an air-breathing mammal or lizard – spending far more time below the surface than above it and, therefore, the plesiosaur theory never made any sense in the first place. He also points out that no fish, as far as we know, has ever evolved a long neck, simply because a fish with gills as opposed to an animal with a complete lung system has no need for such a physical feature. A long neck and two humps seen at a great distance may have been a red deer, 'which is a much more common sight at Loch Ness than many people believe'. Another sighting of a long neck could have been a cormorant. Says Adrian, 'The sighting occurred in the early evening with the witnesses faced directly into the setting sun, which would have culminated in a silhouette effect.'

He has since suggested that brief sightings of a long neck, often described as 'telegraph poles', may be pine logs or sticks momentarily upended in the water due to turbulence. One such sighting by Father Gregory Brusey and Roger Pugh (already outlined) might be explained as just such an example. Adrian points out how they both described the head and neck as it 'collapsed' and 'fell down sideways', rather than dived, which suggests they could have witnessed an inanimate object which behaved in this way.

The Brusey/Pugh sighting is just one of several which have occurred at the mouth of the River Tarfe, near Fort Augustus, and could have been explained by these pine logs being propelled by the force of a violent spate after a heavy rainfall in the river as it emptied into the loch. Steve

Feltham took a video of a stick caught in underwater debris which looked like a head and neck from a distance. BBC newsreader and author of *The Loch Ness Story*, Nicholas Witchell, had a brief glimpse of just such an object, which was gone before he could train his camera on it. He soberly pointed out that he would not accept this as a genuine sighting of an animal from anyone else, so therefore he rejects it himself.

MORE FAKES . . . AND MISTAKES

Adrian Shine is not some arrogant arch-debunker; he has no axe to grind. Diplomatic as he is, he suggests what people have really seen, then leaves them to form their own opinion. 'Just because I offer an alternative theory to account for a sighting, it doesn't necessarily make that theory correct.' However, he does have reservations about some of the 'classic' evidence; not just photographs but cine footage and underwater photography, too.

One such example is the cine film taken by Tim Dinsdale in April 1960. 'Analysts describe it as "a featureless black hump,"' says Adrian. 'But as the object is moving directly away from the camera at a great distance, it cannot be interpreted as anything else. However, watch the object as it turns left to run parallel with the opposite shore, then look directly into the wash behind it. The helmsman of a boat is clearly visible. Not a fake,' says Adrian, 'just a mistake.'

Rip Hepple disagrees. 'I'm sure that Tim didn't film a boat. The wakes are quite dissimilar.'

Another cine film, taken by Peter and Gwen Smith, appears to show a head and neck continually submerging and resurfacing next to a youth sat in a dinghy. Adrian suspects a hoax perpetrated by the youth and his friend who were camped on the shore. 'The object is probably a piece of wood, operated by a length of rope and with rocks used as weights. In fact, it would be quite similar to perception tests devised by the Loch Ness Project to test eyewitnesses.' (Some of these tests are included on film at the new exhibition at the official centre at Drumnadrochit.) He says that the youth was subsequently interviewed on a radio broadcast shortly after the sighting, recalling that 'even though the object had appeared just a few feet away from him, he didn't seem able, or willing, to describe it. He was loath to even say it was an animal of any kind. It would be interesting to contact the man after all this time to see if he would admit to the suspected hoax.'

In his own words, Adrian Shine is 'an underwater man', having spent countless hours exploring underwater conditions in his own self-built bathoscope. Therefore he is less inclined to accept other, often erroneous interpretations of sonar charts and underwater photographs at face value because, 'I know what it's like down there!'

He remains sceptical of the three underwater photographs taken by Dr Bob Rines and the Academy of Applied Sciences. He thinks the diamond-shaped flipper was possibly a close-up shot of a normal-sized fish; the full body shot resembling a plesiosaur could have been formed by shifting silt patterns on the loch bed, and the hideous, gargoyle-like head was probably misidentification of stationary debris.

In later years, Adrian hauled a tree stump to the surface of Urquhart Bay which, it has to be said, greatly resembled the 'head' photo. Nicholas Witchell was there to witness the discovery and, previously excited at the Rines photos, he stated that they should no longer be considered as evidence.

I asked Adrian Shine how something as heavy as a tree stump could drift through open water and past the camera which was suspended in mid-water. He replied that he knew for a fact that the camera in the 1975 expedition had hit the loch bed and was actually rolling around on the bottom, clearly recorded in the LNPIB log book at that time.

FOOD SUPPLY

During the early 1980s, Adrian and the Loch Ness Project manned sonar observation boats and found the entire surface area of the loch was well stocked with fish.

However, is this enough for Nessie? The idea that fish alone, including migratory salmon, could support a colony of large predators would become one of the major issues in the Loch Ness debate. With the fish-count estimate standing at 20 tons – and plant life down to a minimum due to lack of light penetration in the darkened waters – such a small food supply for such a large lake convinced the sceptics that the 'monster' could not exist.

However, retired detective Ian Cameron, who shared the longest-ever recorded sighting with eight other people, told a documentary film team, 'I'm not going to worry about what it feeds on; it could live on fresh air for all I care – because I know that I saw the thing.'

OPERATION DEEPSCAN

In 1987, Shine instigated 'Operation Deepscan', consisting of a flotilla of 20 motor-cruisers strung out across the loch, scanning the depths with sonar. Although many targets were dismissed as stationary debris or shoals of fish, three still remain unexplained to this day.

Patrolling the loch, the team tracked a number of odd targets, including two large objects which were moving together quite close to the surface. The strength of these and other contacts appeared stronger than any of the known fish in Loch Ness encountered on previous trials.

SONAR

It has been suggested that sonar interpretation is ambiguous and therefore more 'art' than 'science' because it doesn't indicate the length of an underwater target.

'True enough,' says Adrian Shine. 'It is ambiguous – but sonar is a science, and while length is not indicated, the strength of contact is. So, for example, when we make a contact we say, "If this is an animal, then, judging by the strength of the contact, it is probably in the order of x metres in length."'

As Nicholas Witchell pointed out in *The Loch Ness Story*, '. . . the sonar charts yielded yet more evidence that Loch Ness is capable of producing mid-water targets which simply should not be there.' Further important work was done to try and ascertain what could cause these heavy sonar traces other than large animals. Thermal currents and side echoes needed to be investigated.

Editor of *Nessletter*, Rip Hepple said, 'One of the problems, I feel, is that sonar is a very imprecise tool – even the present up-to-date equipment.' He recalled how, in 1983, the navies of Norway and Sweden made fleeting contacts with suspect submarines, apparently nosing around their secret naval installations. They trapped them in steep-sided, narrow fjords which '. . . would have been very similar to Loch Ness. Even though they were equipped with very good sonar, the contacts somehow slipped away.' Says Rip, 'This highlights the problem faced by the Project in their work.'

'Ghost targets' or 'rogue blips' may also be produced by a sonar machine itself, which automatically changes scale as the water depth increases, producing such confusing targets. Loch Ness is notorious for creating apparent sonar targets where none exist. The steep mountainsides above the loch drop almost vertically to form this deep, narrow basin of water, which result in echoes bouncing off either side to produce sound waves. These waves are often picked up by sonar – and interpreted as solid objects – but which aren't really anything more than just reverberations.

I asked Adrian Shine if a sidewall echo could continue to be tracked as a possible target for a length of time. He replied that a freak side echo will continue to move in range as the boat is moving.

RINES RETURNS

Despite their opposing views on the mystery, Dr Bob Rines asked Adrian to lend a helping hand on his most recent expedition to the loch in the summer of 1996. Rines was also accompanied by the only remaining member from the original 1970s expedition team, film innovator Charles Weikoff, who sadly died recently. Also joining him were partners in a leading sonar business, American Underwater Search and Survey Ltd, who had volunteered their services to Rines. Not only did Rines want to see if there was still something at the loch worth investigating but, with the aid of oceanographer John Fish and marine biologist Arnie Carr, he would also attempt to track and film underwater targets.

Dr Rines explained his interest in the mystery. 'If you don't have an open mind, in my judgement, you're not a scientist. If you don't have ideas, if you don't have adventure, if you don't have an open mind – you'll never make a discovery.'

The four-day expedition involved some close encounters with what appeared to be large moving targets. 'Have you ever had anything like this before?' asked Arnie Carr, referring to one of the targets. 'No,' replied the helmsman, 'we've never had anything quite as big as that before.' Unfortunately, the target was lost at a depth of around 20 metres, as it passed between the boat's hull and the tow-fish lower down – so the side-scan failed to pick it up.

Arnie Carr, who was initially sceptical of the monster story, later commented, 'I think there's a phenomenon here, or something, that is really interesting, that I would like to get an answer to . . . Now, we had a target today; it didn't look like a thermal to me – it looked more biological – but I don't know what it was.'

The team also achieved a trace on the sonar chart which seemed to be at the bottom of the loch. They made a quick turn in the boat, combing the area again, to find out if it was just stationary debris – and found the target had vanished, indicating that the target had been moving. The nearest the team got to capturing something on film was when they viewed a shoal of salmon through the underwater camera, which they interpreted as being chased by a large predator. However, the target itself was moving too fast to pick up and it was soon lost.

Although his team failed to capture the tracked target on film, Dr Bob Rines concluded, 'If we can intrigue this new generation – and I think we have intrigued – with the work we are doing here, then we will have achieved a great deal.

NESSIE IDENTIKIT

Seldom does a year pass at Loch Ness without several reported sightings and whenever sonar teams set off across the water looking for some trace of the enigma of the loch, they often find it. So what really is the riddle of Loch Ness? Adrian Shine has spent well over two decades seeking an answer to just that question, while answering various other questions about the loch, and separating fact and fantasy in the history of this intriguing puzzle.

What could it be?

Early reports of a giant hippopotamus, a huge frog, a crocodile and an alligator at Loch Ness are clearly examples of mistaken identification. Adrian says that the last two could be explained as sturgeons, which share their scaly, reptilian appearance and, in British waters, can grow up to three metres in length. However, he takes stories of giant eels with a large pinch of salt.

'There is one such story of an eel, measuring eighteen feet long by three feet wide, which allegedly clogged up an intake at the Foyers hydroelectric power station. This has never been substantiated, and giant eels in Loch Ness remain just as elusive as the legendary monster.'

However, sceptical doesn't mean dismissive, and while some sightings can be explained away, there are those which remain. He has stated quite categorically that there is no monster in Loch Ness. A mystery, yes – and one that deserves an explanation – but no mythical monster. 'There is something of zoological interest in Loch Ness,' he says. 'We've known that for years.'

In recent years Adrian has assisted scientists like Dr Roger Jones and his team from Lancaster University with their study of the food-web structure in Loch Ness. With his help, Dr Jones discovered a micro-organism in the silt on the loch bed which was finally accepted in 1996 as a new sub-species of planktonic protozoan. 'Exciting to us,' Dr Jones told me, 'but not likely to grab the public's imagination! This is fundamental freshwater science and has little direct bearing on the Loch Ness monster mystery. I am afraid science may never provide a "solution" to the enigma you refer to. Even if scientific results point logically in one direction, those with real faith will always be willing to look the other way.'

Good point. But what 'solution' can we reasonably expect?

Whatever 'Nessie' turns out to be, Adrian estimates its size at around three metres in length. This seems to tally with sonar contacts measuring around three metres long (other people's estimates include five metres) and Deepscan experts who interpreted targets as 'larger than sharks but smaller than whales'.

So, as writer Jerome Clark put it in his book *Unexplained*: 'Is Nessie merely unusual or truly extraordinary?'

Theories abound and differ widely between researchers.

Steve Feltham is unsure what Nessie could be. He says, 'Whatever it is, it's sure to be something new, if only because you don't usually get things the size of Transit vans swimming around in freshwater lakes!'

Professor Roy Mackal, molecular biologist from the University of Chicago, former Director of Investigations for the LNPIB and author of the scientific tome *The Monsters of Loch Ness*, favours an ancient snake-like whale called the zeugladon (or basilosaurus).

Rip Hepple remains open-minded on the subject, though points out in *Nessletter* that Prof. Mackal's proposed species matches eyewitness descriptions even better than the plesiosaur did. Dr Bob Rines has a similar theory. Considering his underwater flipper photo, he says, 'I think that scientists – as people who earn a living at this – are not ready to believe on the basis of one photograph that something which should have been dead over 65 million years ago is still existing in some form, here at Loch Ness, Scotland.'

And what does Adrian Shine think?

'I wouldn't myself go in for any kind of lizard – Jurassic or otherwise – viable and able to sustain itself here. The loch's waters are very unproductive. So it is a lost world at the bottom of Loch Ness – but it's not Jurassic Park! Possibly we're talking about a large fish.'

And he does not need to justify his own view to anyone.

'I've put 20 years of my life into the search at Loch Ness. I've found my own answer to the mystery and drawn my own conclusions. It may not suit everyone – but it satisfies me.' There is nothing of the 'hard sell' about Adrian Shine – he did not once try to convince me of anything. I asked for his opinion and he gave it – and then left me to make up my own mind. And I have.

There is a very real wildlife mystery waiting to be solved at Loch Ness. Or, as Constance Whyte wrote way back in 1957: '. . . the monster story is a page in the book of nature; an important one perhaps – perhaps not. Some day the truth must surely be known.'

Sixty-seven years after the story first hit the headlines it remains unsolved. But one day, Steve Feltham, Bob Rines, Alistair Boyd, Rip Hepple, or Adrian Shine may just come face to face with Britain's elusive resident – and finally solve the riddle of Loch Ness.

RECENT DEVELOPMENTS

My thanks to independent Loch Ness investigator Richard A. Carter for allowing me access to recent additions to his Loch Ness archives. Richard is a very down-to-earth researcher, with a great interest in the Loch Ness mystery, though remains sceptical of many classic sightings, including 'land sightings', and has, he believes, recreated the famous footage taken by Tim Dinsdale in 1960.

He points out that the original footage shows a local fishing boat – which Dinsdale filmed by mistake under bad light conditions. The boat he filmed two hours later for comparison was taken under entirely brighter conditions, which could account for why the boat and the 'monster' appear to be different.

Way back in August 1972, Commander A.G.W. Bellars and four members of his family saw two 'humps' moving through the waters of Urquhart Bay. Commander Bellars described the objects to me as 'similar to two large elephants standing in shallow water'. Were they boat wakes, as Adrian Shine has suggested that many sightings show, or one of a host of other natural illusions which eyewitnesses have reported for years? Or did they really see Nessie? There have been many sightings in recent years and, since most visitors to Loch Ness carry cameras and, better still, camcorders, various images have been caught and submitted for analysis.

10 APRIL 1994 An unnamed couple reported seeing 'an extremely large object, having two large brown shapes about ten feet in diameter and three feet apart'. It was seen in broad daylight, about 200 yards off the north shore road near Urquhart Castle. The lady said: 'It was definitely an animal of some sort – something came up then went down again.' She said she was amazed that there had been no response from any of the passengers on a pleasure boat which was in Urquhart Bay at the time. 'Somebody must have seen it. It was so big that when I noticed it, it gave me a fright.'

AUGUST 1995 Ian Finlayson was filming his wife, Vera, and their daughter, when they noticed a disturbance out in the loch, and a black shape emerged heading towards the opposite shore. Mrs Finlayson said: 'There were no humps or fins and the creature moved with a twisting movement like a snake. It was very, very long and we estimated that it must have been 30 to 40 feet in length. It wasn't a log, beavers, a school of fish, freak waves or the wake of a boat, this was definitely a solid shape.' After many trips to the loch this was their first sighting of anything strange in the water. She said,, 'I felt privileged to have seen it. I don't know what it was for certain, but I'm quite logical and I would have to say it was a giant eel or something like that.' She added: 'I definitely would not go water-skiing or swimming, in fact I would not even go wading now. Even if it isn't a monster, whatever's out there is quite frightening enough.'

10 APRIL 1996 John and Linda Hedgley and their family were driving along the north shore between Drumnadrochit and Fort William when they saw a head in the water, which appeared solid and jet black, with a massive hump behind it. His wife Linda said: 'We all saw it – whatever it was must have been massive.' John added that although he had been driving along Loch Ness regularly over the last 20 years he had been sceptical previously and had never seen anything untoward.

15 JUNE 1996 Owners of the Craigdarroch House Hotel at Foyers, on the south shore, were among the 16 people who watched a frothy disturbance on the surface of the loch. Kate and David Munro and 14 other people watched the disturbance which moved quickly across the loch before submerging. It never broke the surface, but it sounds like the object had a power source as the wake zig-zagged across the surface as if continually changing direction.

1 AUGUST 1996 Nick Watson, of Lincolnshire, and two other witnesses (names unknown), had quite a convincing sighting from Fort Augustus pier. He said, 'There was a black hump, to the far right of a pleasure yacht, which appeared shiny in the water, at a distance of about one and a half miles, sending a large wake ahead and behind it as it moved up towards the point where I was standing on the pier. It then turned right, then right again, then headed off in the direction of Urquhart Bay. I studied it with my binoculars until it submerged.'

9 AUGUST 1996 The Hutton family from Great Yarmouth took a photograph of an object they had witnessed from the south shoreline between Dores and Foyers. It was definitely an animate object – and the photo of the object is probably genuine – which moved then stopped dead and changed direction.

12 AUGUST 1996 Paul Alexander and his family were on a

pleasure cruise in Urquhart Bay when he saw a large wake in the water. He said, 'Something solid, black and alive, just below the surface seemed to be powering it along at a fair speed in a north-easterly direction, towards Inverness and off Loch Ness.' He added: 'I am not the kind of person to go jumping up and down shouting "I've seen Nessie!", but the rest of the family also saw what I caught on video. I have a science degree, so I need a rational explanation, but I honestly cannot reach a definite conclusion here.'

18 AUGUST 1996 Photographer Craig Kerr took an astounding photograph of a curved line sticking out of the water, which he says he did not see at the time. At first glance it looks even more convincing than the Surgeon's Photograph, though what it really shows has not been established. Certainly the most astounding photo in recent years.

22 AUGUST 1996 Frank Wilson, an angler on his way home from Skye, accompanied by his friend Willie McLean and his two boys, photographed something that appears as a black line on the surface of the water. He said, 'Willie's boys heard a loud whooshing noise 100 yards off the shore, at Invermoriston, and we watched something greyish with two humps and a tail moving rapidly through the water. It appeared with a humped back followed by a flipper raised from the surface. It must have travelled about 300 yards before it disappeared. I was never a believer before, but now I know there's something down there.'

Willie McLean, of Bournemouth, said: 'It was quite remarkable. It looked like a huge snake. I still can't believe it!'

5 SEPTEMBER 1996 Inverness art and photography teacher Austin Hepburn photographed an odd wake from a vantage point between Dores and Torness on the south shore. He said, 'I saw this baffling movement in the water. It lasted for about four minutes and was

travelling northwards a little more than walking pace. I certainly thought I could see something solid causing the unusually shaped wake in the water.' Austin has lived in the area for over 20 years but has never seen anything like this. He said, 'Now, when I look through a magnifying glass at the pictures, I believe I can make out two black humps.'

1 MAY 1998 Mrs Julie Hill, of the West Midlands, was with her husband and two-year-old daughter, staying at the Loch Ness Caravan and Camping Park on the northern shore. With excellent visibility on a warm and sunny day, with the loch water calm, they spotted a dome-like object appear in the water. Mrs Hill said: 'As we looked towards Urquhart Castle from the beach near the site we watched it submerge – but then reappear again, two to three minutes later, having crossed the loch, and it was now nearer the far bank.' Mrs Hill said that the object was definitely animate as it swam and left a wake. It submerged and emerged several times before swimming off towards Urquhart Castle. Each time it submerged it disappeared straight down instead of 'up-ending' and diving. The animal had a long, rounded snout, a large rounded head, dark in colour and its skin or fur shone in the sunlight. 'We estimate that the animal's head was about ten inches long. It was certainly large as it showed up clearly even at about two-thirds of the way across the loch.'

19 JUNE 1998 Mrs Christian Mackintosh-Palmer, of Beauly, saw something appear on the surface of the loch one evening. It appeared in the water opposite the Clansman Hotel at Bracka as she stood on the lower deck of the vessel Jacobite Queen, which takes pleasure cruises on the loch. Said Mrs Mackintosh-Palmer: 'I didn't believe in the monster before but now I know that something definitely exists down there. The loch was completely calm at that time and there was no other boat in sight. It was a big black object that rose out of the water. It was moving quite fast at right angles

to us in the cruiser and had a very clear wake, until it submerged after a few minutes. The part that was visible was only a fraction of the size of the whole creature. I am sure of that. I am certain that the great bulk of it was below the surface. It was an amazing experience. I could hardly believe my eyes when I saw it breaking the calm surface.

MID-1998 The Mitcheson family took a video of a creature with a head and neck, though many have stated quite categorically that it shows a seal, including Dr David Waugh, director-designate of the Royal Zoological Society of Scotland, who studied the film with colleagues. He said, 'We have a very high level of confidence that this was a seal. The next logical option would be an otter. However, there is always room for doubt.' Both Rip Hepple and Neil Willis, a marine biologist from the Sea Life Centre, at Tynemouth, were also convinced that the object was a grey seal.

31 DECEMBER 1998 Lorien Cameron and her fiancé, Kevin Ross, were driving towards Dores from Kindrummond when, as they turned a corner which treated them to a panoramic view of the loch, they saw something opposite Abriachan pier, which shone brightly in the low winter sun. The loch was calm and the weather clear. They saw the shape of a hump reflecting the silvery light of the sun, which they likened to an upturned boat, and watched it for ten to fifteen seconds before it submerged. They added that the object did not seem to move within the duration of the sighting. Their view was obstructed by trees for a short distance, and although they looked for the object again it did not reappear.

24 APRIL 1999 Dave Turner of Southport and his partner Tracy walked up the hill of Inverfarigaig nature trail. Using 10x50 binoculars, Tracy saw what she described as a 'large patch of smooth, black water' and became convinced she could see something under the water.

She said, 'A large dark patch of water caught my eye, so I started looking more closely at the area. I could see the large, dark area of water, then a separate area to the right that appeared to be travelling independently from the stationary large area. This looked like an animate object moving slowly, as if basking, but with the jerky movements of what appeared to be four limbs. It was these limb-like shapes which made me think that this was just a dark patch of water. Neither shape broke the surface and, although size was difficult to judge, I would say it was larger than a small boat. The sighting lasted only for a few minutes.' Tracy told Dave what she was seeing so he trained the camcorder on it, but could find nothing to focus on. When they played back the tape later on, Dave thought he had been looking too far to the left. The time recorded on the tape was 11.25 a.m., the weather was sunny and there was a light wind causing ripples on the surface of the loch.

There were two more vague sightings passed on to me by Rip Hepple and Richard Carter, though each witness refused to give their name. One was similar to the Spicer sighting on the road between Dores and Foyers. In late February 1999, an American tourist reported a long-necked creature between ten and fifteen metres in length which appeared from the dark and scurried into the water! The second was from a lady from Wiltshire who saw a large black object raised from the loch in Urquhart Bay, measuring about ten feet in height. Both of these accounts contain excessive lengths – particularly in the first example.

The Loch Ness monster is not really a 'monster'. It is this word which has caused the subject to be classed as a silly-season joke. In his book *The Loch Ness Story*, Nicholas Witchell sensibly refers to them as the 'Loch Ness animals', but elsewhere fact and fantasy have been rolled into one. Fake photographs, genuine mistakes of wildlife, driftwood and the occasional April Fool pranks have combined to make this subject the butt of much ridicule.

And yet the mystery remains – and the sightings continue.

Zoologist Chris Packham wrote and presented a BBC TV series *The X Creatures*, examining the scientific side of 'mystery animals' such as Nessie and Bigfoot. He and the other experts made several valid points about Nessie, which was surprising as they had never been made public before. He proved that Nessie could not be a reptile – whether a Jurassic aquatic reptile like the plesiosaur or otherwise. The bottom line, of course, is that Nessie has to be a fish rather than an air-breathing animal – because it only very occasionally comes to the surface. The programme helped to dispel many myths which never made sense anyway, but it didn't disprove the existence of Nessie – it only disproved the existence of Nessie as a reptile or mammal.

Eyewitness accounts suggest an animal with a humped back, four flippers and possibly a long neck but which, as we have found, cannot be plesiosaur. So what? Just because it may resemble a plesiosaur, it doesn't necessarily mean that it is a plesiosaur. Giraffes have long necks but they're not plesiosaurs. The physical structure of a long-necked seal would look very similar to a plesiosaur and may even account for some of the land sightings – but they're not plesiosaurs either. Many eyewitnesses say that the head is so tiny it almost seems to be a continuation of the neck – yet the plesiosaur had a very prominent jawbone jutting out from the neck.

The notion that Nessie is a fish would account for the fact that no one has yet gained a decent photograph of it, as it rarely comes to the surface. And the unexplained sonar contacts are the scientific side to the reports – and actually seem to corroborate them.

I am not a zoologist, marine biologist or oceanographer, and I had very little interest in these disciplines before I began my research. Whatever species it may turn out to be, the basic question remains: have people been seeing a large unknown animal in Loch Ness, or have they all been either grossly mistaken or, for some unfathomable reason, blatantly lying, even when many of them decided against reporting their sightings to the press, shunning any kind of publicity for fear of ridicule?

There are historical accounts, too. Not myths and legends, for example the fabled 'water kelpie' or 'water horse', which is the maritime equivalent to the bogeyman, or the 'monster' reported by St Columba in AD 565. The saint may have used this tale to try to persuade the Picts to convert to Christianity, in other words, become Christians or you will be easy prey for evil influences or 'monsters'.

The real historical accounts include a press cutting dating from the nineteenth century, reporting how a 'strange fish' came ashore which drew great crowds of onlookers, and which was buried in the vicinity of the former Lochend Inn. And what of the ancient map-makers' phrase, 'Waves without wind, fish without fin and a floating island', which, although regularly attributed to sightings at Loch Ness, actually originated from Loch Lomond? The earliest recorded 'monster' sighting was at Loch Morar, not Ness. For Loch Ness is not alone in sightings of mysterious creatures – Lochs Awe, Rannoch, Lochy, Morar, Lomond and Llyn Tegid (Lake Bala) in North Wales (and others from around the world) have also had sightings of humped backs, floating islands and long necks breaking the surface.

Perhaps it is significant that these historical accounts sound remarkably similar to the most common sighting at Loch Ness – that of a large, black, rounded object, likened to an upturned boat, which zig-zags across the surface, often moving against the wind currents, implying that it is an animate object with a power source.

Like a detective, readers must strip away all the nonsense that has attached itself to this subject and decide for themselves. Don't take my word for it.

When the Loch Ness mystery is finally solved, it will be viewed in hindsight as a lesson to scientists and to society as a whole. Why had so many people, when often corroborated by others, been dismissed as mad, drunk, liars or charlatans when what they had seen was obviously something very real – when any judge and jury in the land would have accepted such damning mass eyewitness testimony without question?

I am quite sure that the breathtaking area around Loch Ness and Inverness would eventually have attracted me to the area, purely on its own merit, but my main interest is the Loch Ness monster mystery which, contrary to popular opinion, is not pure nonsense. Mark my words: there is something at Loch Ness which has yet to be explained, and that 'something' – regardless of what species it turns out to be – is the very real Loch Ness Monster!

FURTHER READING

Here are some of the books on the subject, but scour your local library and you may find more. The publications by Ronald Binns and Steuart Campbell are 'anti' and take negative and sceptical views of the mystery. The authors support their theories by placing sightings into explainable groups – and anything like close-range sightings which do not fit into a group are ignored. However, they are packed with lots of common sense and help to dispel various myths about the mystery. The book by Richard Frere is mainly about the Loch Ness area and history but includes a good chapter on Nessie.

Bauer, Ronald H., *The Enigma of Loch Ness* (1986, University of Illinois Press)

Binns, Ronald, *The Loch Ness Mystery Solved* (1983, Open Books)

Bord, Janet and Colin, *Alien Animals* (1980, Granada Publishing)

Burton, Maurice, *The Elusive Monster* (1961, Rupert Hart-Davis)

Campbell, E.M., *The Search for Morag* (Loch Morar) (1973, Tom Stacey)

Campbell, Steuart, *The Loch Ness Monster: The Evidence* (1986, The Aquarian Press)

Costello, Peter, *In Search of Lake Monsters* (1973, Garnstone Press)

Dinsdale, Tim, *Loch Ness Monster* (1966, Routledge & Kegan Paul)

The Leviathans (1966, Routledge & Kegan Paul)

Project Water Horse (1975, Routledge & Kegan Paul)

Frere, Richard, *Loch Ness* (1988, John Murray)

Gould, Rupert, *Loch Ness Monster and Others* (1930, Geoffrey Bles)

Holiday, F.W., *The Great Orm of Loch Ness* (1968, Futura Publication)

McEwan, Graham J., *Mystery Animals of Britain and Ireland* (1986, Robert Hale)

Whyte, Constance, *More Than A Legend* (1957, Hamish Hamilton Ltd)

Witchell, Nicholas, *The Loch Ness Story* (1974, Terence Dalton Ltd)

Also, a book specifically about the hoaxed Surgeon's Photograph, strongly recommended for those with an interest in the origins of one of the most famous photographic images in the world, written by zoologist Dave Martin and experienced Loch Ness researcher Alistair Boyd, who have appeared on TV documentaries *The Secrets of Loch Ness* and *Return to Loch Ness*: *Nessie: The Surgeon's Photograph Exposed.*

Tel: (0181) 440 4554 for more details.

PERIODICALS

Nessletter, R.R. Hepple, 7 Huntshieldford, St John's Chapel, Weardale, Co Durham DL13 1RQ. Tel: (01388) 537359. Subscriptions (per year or at least six issues): UK £2.75; North America $10.00.

Fortean Times, which covers almost every mystery or strange happening reported from around the world. Readers act as correspondents by sending in relevant press cuttings (including date, source and name if you want crediting). Available in newsagents. Address: Bob Rickard and Paul Sieveking (editors), Box 2409, London NW5 4NP.

PART 2: INVERNESS

GENERAL INFORMATION

CAR PARKS

CASTLE STREET (C3)

There is a car park in the shadow of Inverness Castle – on Castle Street take first right turn past McDonald's, from the town centre.

EASTGATE SHOPPING CENTRE (D2)

See Academy Street (C2), turn right under shoppers' footbridge and left under a second footbridge, and the multi-storey car park is on your left.

INVERNESS RAILWAY STATION

Opposite Eastgate Shopping Centre, on the right of Falcon Square (C2).

ROSE STREET

See Rose Street – off Academy Street – to the left of Farraline Park bus station (C2).

PUBLIC TRANSPORT

INVERNESS RAILWAY STATION

Station Square, Inverness (C3). Tel 08457 48 49 50 (national rail enquiries), see car park mentioned above.

FARRALINE PARK BUS STATION

Margaret Street, Inverness (C3). Tel (01463) 233371. Please note: Margaret Street is a one-way street, so if you are approaching by car, then the best approach is along Strother's Lane, to the right of Margaret Street, then take the first turn into the bus station.

BANKS AND BUILDING SOCIETIES

Most branches in Inverness have cash dispensers of their own – some don't – but most are in walking distance of each other, so you should never find yourself short of cash.

ABBEY NATIONAL
Tel 0845 765 4321
1 Union Street (C2)
Link cash dispenser

ALLIANCE & LEICESTER
Tel (01463) 242136
32 Eastgate (C3)
Link cash dispenser

BANK OF SCOTLAND
Tel (01463) 882000
9 High Street (C3)
Link cash dispenser

CLYDESDALE BANK
Tel (01463) 221791
15 Academy Street (C2)
Link cash dispenser

CLYDESDALE BANK
Tel (01463) 222727
32 Longman Road (C1)
Link cash dispenser

CLYDESDALE BANK
Tel (01463) 239167
Raigmore Hospital (See
Damfield Road (D4/E4),
follow on to Culcabock Road,
continue on to Old Perth
Road, turn left at the ring road
on to Sir Walter Scott Drive
and the entrance to the hos-

pital is the first left turning.)
Link cash dispenser

DUNFERMLINE BUILDING
SOCIETY
Tel (01463) 241071
15 Bridge Street (C3)
No cash dispenser

LLOYDS TSB
Tel (01463) 713738
39-41 Union Street (C2)
Link – two cash dispensers

NORTHERN ROCK
Tel (01463) 221781
7-19 Lombard Street (C3) –
between Baron Taylor's Street
and High Street
No cash dispenser

THE ROYAL BANK OF
SCOTLAND
Tel (01463) 236363
25 Queensgate (C2)
Link cash dispenser

THE ROYAL BANK OF
SCOTLAND
Tel (01463) 236363
17 Tomnahurich Street (B3)
Link cash dispenser

THE ROYAL BANK OF
SCOTLAND
Tel (01463) 236363
29 Harbour Road (D1) There
are two parts to Harbour
Road, follow Longman Road
out of the town centre and
take the right turning.
Link cash dispenser

WOOLWICH
Tel (01463) 242000

19a Union Street (C2)
Link cash dispenser

YORKSHIRE BUILDING
SOCIETY
Tel (01463) 222772
25 Inglis Street (C2/C3)
between Academy Street and
High Street
No cash dispenser

POST OFFICES & SUB POST OFFICES

INVERNESS MAIN POST
OFFICE
Tel (01463) 243574
14 Queensgate (C2)

TOMNAHURICH STREET PO
Tel (01463) 231410
Tomnahurich Street (B3)

CULDUTHEL PO
Tel (01463) 230532
114 Culduthel Road (C4)

DALNEIGH PO
Tel (01463) 231955
30 Laurel Avenue (A4/A3)

KINGSMILLS ROAD PO
Tel (01463) 233038
6 Southside Road (C4/D4)

MUIRTOWN PO
Tel (01463) 233483
89-91 Telford Street (A2)

PETROL STATIONS
All Inverness petrol filling stations have shops and you don't
need to have purchased petrol to use them. Some are open all
night, others close late.

BLACKPARK FILLING STATION
Tel (01463) 233632
See Telford Street (A2),
continue along Telford Street,
crossing the Muirtown Bridge
and continue on to
Clachnaharry Road.

Shop open 7 a.m. – 10 p.m.

CROMWELL'S TOWER
FILLING STATION
Tel (01463) 220011
Chapel Street (B2)

FRIAR'S BRIDGE FILLING
STATION
Tel (01463) 220555
16 Telford Street (A2)
Shop open all night

HIGHLANDER SERVICE
STATION
Tel (01463) 242122
Millburn Road (D2)
Shop open 7 a.m. – 11.30
p.m.

MILLERTON FILLING
STATION
Tel (01463) 232086

Glenurquhart Road (A5)
Shop open 7 a.m. – 10 p.m.

RAIGMORE SERVICE
STATION
Tel (01463) 236663
Millburn Road (D2)
Shop open all night

SHELL KINGSWELL
Tel (01463) 245930
See Damfield Road (D4/B4),
follow Damfield Road on to
Culcabock Road, continue on
to Old Perth Road.
Shop open 7 a.m. – 11 p.m.

INFORMATION

TOURIST INFORMATION
CENTRE
Castle Wynd (off Bridge
Street), Inverness IV2 3BJ
Tel (01463) 234353
Fax (01463) 710609
On Bridge Street (C3), facing
Inverness Castle, take the steps
up to the walkway on the
right. Entrance on left
through swing doors, or
straight on along walkway,
down slope, and second
entrance is on the left through
swing doors.

INVERNESS LIBRARY
(lending library and Highland
archives)

Farraline Park (off Margaret
Street (C2)), Inverness IV1
1NH
Tel (01463) 220330
Fax (01463) 711128
Open all year

MORAY FIRTH RADIO
PO Box 271, Inverness IV3
6SF
Tel (01463) 224433
Fax (01463) 243224
Local independent radio
station, with 24-hour
broadcasting of information
on local events and news.
Wide range of entertainment
to suit everyone. FM 97.4;
MW 1107

AIRPORT

DALCROSS AIRPORT
Dalcross, Ardersier, Inverness
Tel (01463) 462485
Directions See Millburn Road (B865) (D2), follow to the ring road, passing under the flyover roads, join opposite road (A96 trunk road) to Nairn, take the first left turning on to the B9039, towards Dalcross Airport.

PUBLIC CONVENIENCES

INVERNESS CASTLE
Castle Wynd (between Bridge Street and Castle Street) (C3) Between Mealmarket Close and Inglis Street, off Eastgate (C3/C2)

INVERNESS RAILWAY STATION (C2)

FARRALINE PARK BUS STATION
Margaret Street (C2)

EASTGATE SHOPPING CENTRE
Multi-storey car park (C2/D2)

MARKET BRAE
off Eastgate (C3). Follow a narrow flight of steps, WCs are on your right-hand side.

EMERGENCY SERVICES

EMERGENCIES ONLY
National Emergency Services telephone number: 999. State either Fire, Police, Ambulance or Coastguard, speak clearly giving your name and location and other details as required.

POLICE
Queensgate (C2), off Academy Street, opposite Strother's Lane
Tel (01463) 715555

POLICE (STATION)
Old Perth Road, Inverness
Tel (01463) 715555
Directions See Annfield Road (D4). Turn left on to Damfield Road, continue along Culcabock Road, straight on to Old Perth Road (B9006), the police station is on the right-hand side, just before you reach the ring road.

HOSPITAL CASUALTY DEPARTMENT

If you are injured but it is not an emergency and can make your own way there, the casualty department is at Raigmore Hospital, off Sir Walter Scott Drive.

Tel (01463) 704000

Directions From Annfield Road (D4) turn left on to Damfield Road, continue on to Culcabock Road, continue past road island on to Old Perth Road, take the fourth left turn at the ring road on to Sir Walter Scott Drive, take the first left turn to Raigmore Hospital.

WHERE TO STAY

As befits a district which is very popular with holidaymakers, Inverness and Loch Ness offer a wide variety of accommodation. Hotels, guest houses, B&Bs, camping and caravan parks, student/youth hostels and self-catering accommodation are all available in this part of the Highlands. All entries are listed alphabetically.

VER OR NON-VER FACILITIES Each entry details **Ver** facilities (i.e. those facilities that have been verified by inspectors from the Highlands of Scotland Tourist Board) and **Non-ver** facilities (i.e. those facilities which the establishments claim to provide – but which are non-verified). Please telephone, fax or write for full details of facilities – this guide only includes the main ones, e.g. TV, tea/coffee facilities, private parking, smoking/non-smoking.

COMMENTS 'Comments' are by the establishment's proprietors or the Highlands of Scotland Tourist Board. 'Recommendations' are by myself or someone who has visited the places.

EN-SUITE/PRIVATE FACILITIES En-suite means that the bathroom is a separate room but attached on to your own personal room. Private facility is also solely for the use of the individual guest, but is situated away from the guest rooms – possibly across the landing or down the hallway – to which the guest has private access and a private door key for the duration of their stay.

HOTELS/GUEST HOUSES/ BED & BREAKFASTS The Scottish Tourist Board has made the three following classifications
A **hotel** will normally have a minimum of six letting bedrooms, half of which must have en-suite or private bathroom facilities, have a drinks (liquor) licence and offer to serve both breakfast and an evening meal. A **guest house** is

usually a commercial business, normally with a minimum of four letting rooms (some en-suite or private bathroom facilities). Breakfast is always available and often evening meals. A **bed and breakfast** is normally a private house, with usually no more than six bedrooms, offering breakfast, but an evening meal may or may not be available.

SCOTTISH TOURIST BOARD RATINGS Hotels, bed and breakfasts, guest houses and self-catering accommodation have been awarded a star rating. With self-catering accommodation, where there is more than one property on offer (i.e. houses, cottages, apartments, flats, caravans, log cabins), there may be more than one star rating. Hostels have no star rating. Caravan and camping parks are rated with 'ticks' as opposed to 'stars'.

HOTEL BOOKING AGENTS

Hotel & Travel Reservations Ltd

Station Concourse, Academy Street, Inverness

Tel (01463) 715285

Other services available Car hire; sightseeing tours; theatre; concert and sport tickets; Interflora; City Breaks.

Location Academy Street (C2), also an office at Dalcross Airport.

BED AND BREAKFAST

AMULREE

40 Fairfield Road, Inverness IV3 5QD

Tel (01463) 224822

Open All year

Rooms 2 singles, 1 double, 1 twin, 3 en-suite.

Prices B&B – single, £17–£21; double/twin, £17–£22; B&B plus evening meal, £26–£32.

Ver TV in room; tea/coffee facilities; non-smoking; limited parking spaces; TV in lounge.

Non-ver Packed lunches; pets welcome; vegetarian/special diets by arrangement.

Location Fairfield Road (A3).

Directions To Fairfield Road from Ness Bridge (Map 1 – C3), follow along Young Street and Tomnahurich Street, out of town centre, take the fourth right turn to Kenneth Street, follow along, take the second left to Fairfield Road.

STB rating B&B ***

65 Fairfield Road, Inverness IV3 5LH

Tel (01463) 240673

Open November to September

Rooms 1 double, 1 twin, 1 family, 1 en-suite, 1 private facility.

Prices B&B – double/twin, £13 – £17.

Ver TV in room; tea/coffee facilities; non-smoking; limited parking space.

Location Fairfield Road (A3).

Directions To Fairfield Road from Ness Bridge (C3), follow along Young Street and Tomnahurich Street, out of town centre, take the fourth right turn to Kenneth Street, follow along, take the second left to Fairfield Road.

STB rating B&B **

5 Abertarff Road, Inverness IV2 3NW

Tel (01463) 235674

Open All year

Rooms 1 double, 2 family, 3 en-suite.

Prices B&B – double/twin, £18–£22.

Ver TV in room; tea/coffee facilities; non-smoking; private parking; pay phone available.

Non-ver Use of shower; packed lunches by arrangement.

Location Abertarff Road (D2).

Directions To Abertarff Road from Ness Bridge (C3), follow Bank Road, turn right to Friar's Lane, turn right to Academy Street, turn right at Eastgate Centre passing under the shoppers' footbridge, turn left passing under second footbridge, follow to Crown Road, take first right turn to Crown Circus, take first left turn to Abertarff Road.

STB rating B&B ***

42 Fairfield Road, Inverness IV3 5QD

Tel (01463) 240240

Open All year

Rooms 2 single, 2 double, 4 en-suite.

Prices B&B – single, £18–£20; double/twin, £18–£20.

Ver TV in room; tea/coffee facilities; non-smoking; private parking; pay phone available.

Non-ver Use of shower; baby's cot; vegetarian/special diets available by arrangement.

Location Fairfield Road (A3).

Directions To Fairfield Road from Ness Bridge (C3), follow along Young Street and Tomnahurich Street, out of town centre, take the fourth right turn to Kenneth Street, follow along, take the second left to Fairfield Road.

STB rating B&B ***

AVISH

80 Telford Road, Inverness IV3 6HN

Tel (01463) 240502

Open All year

Rooms 2 single, 1 double, 1 twin.

Prices B&B – single, £11–£15; double/twin, £11–£15; B&B plus evening meal, £17–£21.

Ver TV in room; tea/coffee facilities; non-smoking; private parking; pay phone available.

Location Telford Road, off Telford Street (B2).

Directions To Telford Road from Ness Bridge (C3), follow along Young Street and Tomnahurich Street, out of town centre, take the fourth right turn to Kenneth Street, follow along to ring road, drive straight forward to Telford Street, and take second turn on the right to Telford Road. Note that Telford Road is a one-way street and can only be entered from Telford Street.

STB rating B&B *

MRS H.M. BOYNTON

12 Annfield Road, Inverness IV2 3HX

Tel (01463) 233188

Open All year

Rooms 1 double, 1 family.

Prices B&B – double/twin, £15.

Ver TV in room; tea/coffee facilities; private parking; pay phone available.

Location Annfield Road (D4).

Directions Ness Bridge (C3), follow High Street to Castle Street, to Culduthel Road, take first left turn to Old Edinburgh Road, take second left turn to Annfield Road.
STB rating B&B **

BRAEMORE GUESTHOUSE

1 Victoria Drive, Inverness IV2 3QB
Tel (01463) 243318
Open All year
Rooms 1 single, 3 double, 1 twin, 1 family, all en-suite.
Prices B&B – single, £35–£40; double/twin, £25–£27.50.
Ver TV in room; tea/coffee facilities; non-smoking; private parking; use of hairdryer.
Non-ver Use of iron; shower; clothes-drying facilities; vegetarian and special diets and packed lunches by arrangement.
Location Victoria Drive (D2).
Directions Ness Bridge (C3), follow Bank Street, turn right to Friar's Lane, turn right to Academy Street, follow along past Eastgate, on to Millburn Road, take first right turn to Victoria Drive.
Comments Victorian villa furnished with antiques and interesting artefacts. An excellent base from which to explore the neighbouring countryside and to visit many sites of historical interest. Ample private parking available.
STB rating B&B ****

CAMBETH LODGE

49 Fairfield Road, Inverness IV3 5QP
Tel (01463) 231764
Open All year
Rooms 1 double, 2 twin, 1 en-suite.
Prices B&B – double/twin, £15–£10.
Ver TV in room; tea/coffee facilities; non-smoking; private parking; use of hairdryer and pay phone available; TV in lounge.
Location Fairfield Road (A3).
Directions To Fairfield Road from Ness Bridge (C3), follow Young Street and Tomnahurich Street, away from town centre, take fourth right to Kenneth Street, take second left turn to Fairfield Road.
STB rating B&B **

MRS L. CAMERON
Tay Villa, 40 Harrowden Road, Inverness IV3 5QN
Tel (01463) 232984
Open February to mid-December
Rooms 1 double, 1 twin, 2 en-suite.
Prices B&B – double/twin, £16–£17.
Ver TV in room; tea/coffee facilities; non-smoking; pay phone available; TV in lounge.
Location Harrowden Road (A2).
Directions To Harrowden Road from Ness Bridge, follow Young Street and Tomnahurich Street, away from town centre, take fourth right turn at Kenneth Street, take second left turn to Fairfield Road, take fourth right turn to Harrowden Road.
STB rating B&B ***

CARBISDALE
43 Charles Street, Inverness IV2 3AH
Tel (01463) 225689   *Fax* (01463) 225689
Open All year
Rooms 2 double, 1 twin.
Prices B&B – double/twin, £16.
Ver TV in room; tea/coffee facilities; non-smoking; hairdryer available.
Non-ver Use of iron; shower and clothes-drying facilities. Vegetarian and special diets available by arrangement.
Location Charles Street (C3)
Directions From Ness Bridge (C3) follow Bridge Street, turn right to Castle Street, follow on to Culduthel Road, take left turn to Old Edinburgh Road, take first left turn to Mitchell's Lane, take first right turn to Argyle Street, take first left turn to Denny Street, ignore turns to Crown Street and Hill Street and continue to Charles Street.
STB rating B&B ****

MRS S.N. CHALMERS
Tamarue, 70a Ballifeary Road, Inverness IV3 5PF
Tel (01463) 239724
Open January to December
Rooms 1 single, 2 double, 1 private facility.
Prices B&B – double/twin, £13.50–£20.

Ver Tea/coffee facilities; non-smoking; limited parking.

Location Ballifeary Road (A5).

Directions From Ness Bridge (C3), follow Young Street and Tomnahurich Street, away from town centre, continue to Glenurquhart Road, take first left turn to Bishop's Road, and sharp right turn to Ballifeary Road.

STB rating B&B **

CLACH MHUILLINN

7 Harris Road, Inverness IV2 3LS

Tel (01463) 237059   *Fax* (01463) 242092

E-mail elsmlie@globalnet.co.uk

Website www.users.globalnet.co.uk/-elmslie

Open March to November

Rooms 1 double, 1 twin/triple suite, 2 en-suite.

Prices B&B – double/twin, £23–£28.

Ver TV in room; tea/coffee facilities; non-smoking; private parking; use of hairdryer.

Non-ver Use of shower; iron; vegetarian and special diets available; credit/debit cards accepted.

Location Harris Road (E5).

Directions From Ness Bridge (C3) follow Bridge Street, turn right to Castle Street, follow route to Culduthel Road, take left turn on to Old Edinburgh Road, follow on, ignoring left turn to Annfield Road, then take first left turn to Damfield Road, and take second right turn to Harris Road.

Comments En-suite bedrooms with TV, flowers, tea/coffee, etc. Breakfasts served overlooking garden. Credit cards accepted.

STB rating B&B ****

THE COTTAGE

6a Bruce Gardens, Inverness IV3 5EN

Tel (01463) 240253   *Fax* (01463) 240253

Open April to mid-October

Rooms 1 double, 1 twin, 2 en-suite.

Prices B&B – double/twin, £23–£25.

Ver TV in room; tea/coffee facilities; non-smoking; private parking; use of hairdryer.

Non-ver Use of shower and iron; baby's cot; credit/debit cards accepted.

Location Bruce Gardens (A4).

Directions From Ness Bridge (C3) follow Young Street and Tomnahurich Street away from town centre, follow route on to Glenurquhart Road, take first right turn on to Bruce Gardens.

Comments A warm welcome awaits you in this modern cottage where the rooms have been designed with guests' comfort in mind. There is off-the-road parking and is situated in a residential area, ten minutes' walk from the town centre.

STB rating *****

MRS A. DAVIDSON
Balthangie B&B, 37 Ballifeary Lane, Inverness IV3 5PH
Tel (01463) 237637   *Fax* (01463) 224780
E-mail les.d@zetnet.co.uk
Open All year
Rooms 2 double, 1 twin, 3 en-suite.
Prices B&B – double/twin, £20–£24.
Ver TV in room; tea/coffee facilities; non-smoking; private parking; pay phone available; use of hairdryer.
Non-ver Use of iron and clothes-drying facilities; pets welcome by arrangement; credit/debit cards accepted; vegetarian and special diets available; packed lunches available by arrangement.
Location (B4).
Directions From Ness Bridge (C3) follow Young Street and Tomnahurich Street, and follow on to Glenurquhart Road, take second left turn on to Ballifeary Lane.
STB rating B&B ***

DIONARD GUEST HOUSE
39 Old Edinburgh Road, Inverness IV2 3HJ
Tel (01463) 233557   *Fax* (01463) 710526
Open All year
Rooms 2 double, 1 twin, 3 en-suite.
Prices B&B – double/twin, £20–£24.
Ver TV in room; tea/coffee facilities; non-smoking; private parking; pay phone available.
Non-ver Use of shower and iron.
Location Old Edinburgh Road (D4).
Directions From Ness Bridge (C3) follow Bridge Street, turn right

into Castle Street, then straight on to Culduthel Road, then take first left turn to Old Edinburgh Road.

STB rating B&B ***

MRS I. DONALD
4 Muirfield Road, Inverness IV2 4AY
Tel (01463) 235489   *Fax* (01463) 235489
Open All year, except Christmas and New Year.
Rooms 3 double/twin/family, 2 en-suite, 1 private facility.
Prices B&B – double/twin, £19–£21.
Ver Tea/coffee facilities; TV in lounge; non-smoking; private parking; evening meal available if required; use of hairdryer.
Non-ver Use of shower; iron and drying facilities.
Location Muirfield Road (D5).
Directions From Ness Bridge (C3) follow Bridge Street, turn right on to Castle Street, continue route to Culduthel Road, look out for Mackenzie Centre and Woodlands Centre on the left, then take third left turn past there on to Muirfield Road.

STB rating B&B ****

EDEN LODGE (Mrs Jean MacRury)
13 Bishop's Road, Inverness IV3 5SB
Tel (01463) 232999
Open All year
Rooms 1 single, 1 double, 1 family, 3 en-suite.
Prices B&B – single, £20–£24; double/twin, £20–£23.
Ver TV in room; tea/coffee facilities; non-smoking; private parking; use of hairdryer and iron.
Location Bishop's Road (B4).
Directions From Ness Bridge take first left turn at the end of the bridge, away from the town centre, into Ness Walk, follow the route on to Bishop's Road, which continues its course with a turn to the right, eventually leading to Glenurquhart Road.
Comments Eden Lodge is a family run B&B, ten minutes' walk from the town centre and one minute's walk from Eden Court Theatre. Private parking.

STB rating B&B ***

MRS M. EDWARDS
St Kilda, 28 Rangemore Road, Inverness IV3 5EA

Tel (01463) 235200

Open All year

Rooms 1 single, 1 double, 1 family.

Prices B&B – single, £15–£16; double/twin, £14–£16.

Ver TV in room; tea/coffee facilities; non-smoking; use of iron and hairdryer.

Location Rangemore Road (A3).

Directions From Ness Bridge (C3) follow Young Street on to Tomnahurich Street and continue on this route, then take fourth turning on the right on to Montague Row, then take first turning on the left on to Rangemore Road.

STB rating **

MRS J. FIDDES

The Tilt, Old Perth Road, Inverness IV2 3UT

Tel (01463) 225352   *Fax* (01463) 225352

Open All year

Rooms 1 single, 1 twin, 1 family.

Prices B&B – single from £16; double/twin from £14; family from £14.

Ver TV in room; tea/coffee facilities; non-smoking; private parking; pay phone available; use of iron.

Directions From the town centre side of Ness Bridge (C3) take right turn along Bank Street, take right turn along Friar's Lane, take right turn along Academy Street, follow this route on to Millburn Road, continue this route to the ring road, then take right turn on to Old Perth Road.

STB rating B&B ***

MRS H. FINDLAY

Mary Ann Villa, Mary Ann Court, Ardross Place, Inverness IV3 5BZ

Tel (01463) 230187

Open All year

Rooms 1 single, 1 twin, 1 family.

Prices B&B – single, £14–£17; double/twin, £12–£15.

Ver TV in room; tea/coffee facilities; non-smoking; private parking; use of iron; pay phone available.

Location Ardross Place (B3).

Directions From Ness Bridge (C3) follow Young Street, away from

town centre, take second left turning after Ness Bridge on to Alexander Place, take first right on to Ardross Place.
STB rating B&B **

MRS DOREEN GANDER

Canmore, 3 Heathcote Gardens, Muirfield Road, Inverness IV2 4AZ
Tel (01463) 230228
Open All year
Rooms 1 double, 1 twin, 1 en-suite, 1 private facility.
Prices B&B – double/twin, £21.
Ver TV in room; tea/coffee facilities; non-smoking; private parking; use of lounge; hairdryer and iron.
Non-ver Use of shower; clothes-drying facilities; vegetarian and special diets available; credit/debit cards accepted.
Location Heathcote Gardens (C4/C5).
Directions From Ness Bridge (C3) follow Bridge Street, take a right turn on to Castle Street, take the first left turn on to Old Edinburgh Road, take the second right turn on to Muirfield Road, then right on to Heathcote Gardens.
STB rating B&B ****

MRS A. GORDON

12 Mayfield Road, Inverness IV2 4AE
Tel (01463) 231336   *E-mail* ago7195587@aol.com
Open All year
Rooms 2 double, 2 twin, 4 en-suite.
Prices B&B – single, £25–£28; double/twin, £17.50–£19.
Ver TV in room; tea/coffee facilities; non-smoking; private parking; pay phone available; TV in lounge; use of hairdryer.
Non-ver Use of shower; iron; clothes-drying facilities; vegetarian and special diets available; packed lunches by arrangement.
Location Mayfield Road (C4).
Directions To Mayfield Road from Ness Bridge (C3) follow Bridge Street, turn right on to Castle Street, continue on to Culduthel Road, take the second left turn on to Mayfield Road.
Comments Well-appointed, traditionally built Scottish bungalow, situated in a large secluded garden in a pleasant residential area. It has a warm and friendly atmosphere and is only a few

minutes' walk from the town centre, tourist office, River Ness and Inverness Castle.

STB rating B&B ***

HAZELDEAN HOUSE

125 Lochalsh Road, Inverness IV3 5QS

Tel (01463) 241338

Open All year

Rooms 2 double, 1 twin.

Prices B&B – single, £14–£20; double/twin, £14 –£18.

Ver TV in room; tea/coffee facilities; non-smoking; pay phone available; TV in lounge; use of iron.

Non-ver Use of shower; pets welcome by arrangement.

Location Lochalsh Road (A2)

Directions From Ness Bridge (C3) follow Young Street to Tomnahurich Street, away from the town centre, then turn right at Kenneth Street, take a left turn on to Fairfield Road, then take the fifth right turning on to Lochalsh Road. Hazeldean House is about 200 yards down. Please note that this part of Lochalsh Road is a one-way street and can only be accessed from Fairfield Road – not Telford Street.

Personal recommendation If the STB award were based on the number of letters received from satisfied guests who return again and again, then Hazeldean House would have a considerably higher star rating. George and Hazel Stuart are a friendly and accommodating couple, who will make sure that you not only enjoy your stay there, but will recommend the best sights and the best places to eat. Warmly recommended!

STB rating B&B ***

HEBRIDES B&B

(Brenda and Kenneth MacDonald), 120a Glenurquhart Road, Inverness IV3 5TD

Tel (01463) 220062

Open All year

Rooms 2 double (en-suite), 1 twin (private facility).

Prices B&B – £18–£25.

Ver TV in room; tea/coffee facilities; non-smoking; private parking; use of hairdryer and iron.

Location Glenurquhart Road (A5).

Directions From Ness Bridge (C3) follow Young Street and Tomnahurich Street, away from town centre, until the route becomes Glenurquhart Road.

Comments Attractive non-smoking B&B with off-street parking. Adjacent to sports centre, Loch Ness cruises, Caledonian Canal and golf course.

STB rating B&B ****

HIGHFIELD HOUSE

62 Old Edinburgh Road, Inverness IV2 3PG

Tel (01463) 258892   *Fax* (01463) 233892

Open February to November

Rooms 1 double, 1 family.

Prices B&B – double/twin, £17.

Ver TV in room; tea/coffee facilities; non-smoking; private parking; pay phone available; TV in lounge; use of hairdryer.

Non-ver Use of shower; baby's cot; clothes-drying facilities; vegetarian and special diets available.

Location Old Edinburgh Road (D4).

Directions From Ness Bridge (C3) follow Bridge Street, turn right on to Castle Street, take the first left turning on to Old Edinburgh Road.

Comments Situated in a quiet area. Ten minutes' walk from the town centre, this family-run B&B offers quality accommodation, a friendly atmosphere and warm Scottish hospitality. Private off-road parking; non-smoking; tasteful décor throughout. Ideal for golf, fishing, walking or touring.

STB rating B&B ****

MRS J.M. HOGG

21 Crown Drive, Inverness IV2 3QF

Tel (01463) 232614

Open All year

Rooms 1 single, 1 double, 1 twin, 1 en-suite.

Prices B&B – single, £16–£22; double/twin, £16–£24.

Ver TV in room; tea/coffee facilities; non-smoking; private parking.

Location Crown Drive (D2).

Directions From Ness Bridge turn right on to Bank Street, turn right on to Friar's Lane, turn right on to Academy Street, turn right past the Eastgate Centre, passing under two footbridges, turn left on to Crown Road, continue on this route to reach Crown Drive.

STB rating B&B ***

THE KEMPS

64 Telford Street, Inverness IV3 5LS

Tel (01463) 235780

Open All year

Rooms 2 single, 1 double, 1 twin, 3 en-suite, 1 private facility.

Prices B&B – single, £18; double/twin, £18.

Ver TV in room; tea/coffee facilities; non-smoking; private parking; TV in lounge; use of iron.

Non-ver Use of shower; pets welcome by arrangement.

Location Telford Street (A2).

Directions From Ness Bridge (C3) follow Young Street and Tomnahurich Street, turn right on to Kenneth Street, follow straight through the ring road on to Telford Street.

STB rating B&B ***

MRS H. KENNEDY

Kendon, 9 Old Mill Lane, Inverness IV2 3XP

Tel (01463) 238215

Open March to October

Rooms 2 double, 1 twin, 3 en-suite.

Prices B&B – double/twin, £20–£24.

Ver TV in room; tea/coffee facilities; non-smoking; private parking; TV in lounge; use of hairdryer.

Non-ver Packed lunches by arrangement; vegetarian and special diets available.

Location Near Harris Road (E5).

Directions From Ness Bridge (C3) follow Bridge Street, turn right on to Castle Street, turn left on to Old Edinburgh Road, continue past Annfield Road turn-off and take next left turn on to Damfield Road, take second right turning on to Harris Road, at Harris Road junction turn left on to Old Mill Lane.

Comments Enjoy a warm welcome and a restful break in this family-run bungalow, situated in a peaceful location. Lovely garden and driveway for easy parking. An ideal base for touring the Highlands. No smoking throughout this property.

STB rating B&B ***

MRS P. KENNEDY

7 Broadstone Park, Inverness IV2 3JZ

Tel (01463) 236807

Open January to December

Rooms 1 double, 2 twin.

Prices B&B – single, £17; double/twin, £17.

Ver Tea/coffee facilities; TV in lounge; use of iron.

Location Broadstone Park (D3).

Directions From Ness Bridge (C3) follow Bridge Street, turn right on to Castle Street, turn left on to Old Edinburgh Road, turn left on to Southside Road, turn a sharp right on to Kingsmills Road, turn left on to Broadstone Park.

STB rating B&B **

LEINSTER LODGE GUEST HOUSE

27 Southside Road, Inverness IV2 4XA

Tel (01463) 233311

Open All year

Rooms 1 single, 2 double, 1 twin, 1 family, 2 en-suite.

Prices B&B – single, £19–£21; double/twin, £18–£20.

Ver TV in room; tea/coffee facilities; non-smoking; private parking; pay phone available.

Location Southside Road (C4)

Directions From Ness Bridge (C3) follow Bridge Street, turn right on to Castle Street, continue on to Culduthel Road, take the third left turn turning on to Southside Road.

STB rating B&B *

MR AND MRS LEWTHWAITE

Strathisla, 42 Charles Street, Inverness IV2 3AH

Tel (01463) 235657   *Fax* (01463) 235657

Open All year

Rooms 2 single, 1 double, 1 twin.

Prices B&B – single, £16–£20; double/twin, £15–£18; B&B plus evening meal, £23–£28.

Ver TV in room; tea/coffee facilities; non-smoking; limited parking; pay phone in room.

Non-ver Use of shower; vegetarian and special diets available.

Location Charles Street (C3).

Directions From Ness Bridge (C3) follow Bridge Street, turn right

on to Castle Street, turn left on to Old Edinburgh Road, turn left on to Mitchell's Lane, turn right on to Argyle Street, turn left on to Denny Street past Crown Street and Hill Street, turn on to Charles Street.

Comments Built in 1860, this comfortable Victorian house has been tastefully modernised and decorated to a high standard. Two minutes' walk to the town centre and five minutes' walk to the bus station. Warm Scottish hospitality and a homely atmosphere. Off-street parking, no pets and no smoking assures your comfort. Evening meal available by arrangement. Ideal base for touring the highlands. Chinese spoken.

STB rating B&B **

LORNE HOUSE (Mrs U. Moffat)
40 Crown Drive, Inverness IV2 3QG
Tel (01463) 236271
Open All year
Rooms 1 double, 1 family, 1 en-suite, 1 private facility.
Prices B&B – from £17–£25; en-suite, £20–£25.
Ver TV in room; tea/coffee facilities; non-smoking; private parking; pay phone available; use of hairdryer and iron.
Location Crown Drive (D2).
Directions From Ness Bridge (C3) turn right down Bank Street, turn right on to Friar's Lane, turn right on to Academy Street, follow the route to the Eastgate Shopping Centre, take a sharp right under the shopping centre footbridges to follow Crown Road, and follow the same route on to Crown Drive.
STB rating B&B ****

MRS C.A. MACDONALD
14 Glenburn Drive, Inverness IV2 4ND
Tel (01463) 238832   *Fax* (01463) 238832
Open May to September
Rooms 1 single, 1 twin.
Prices B&B – single, £13–£17; double/twin, £12–£16.
Ver TV in room; tea/coffee facilities; non-smoking.
Location Glenburn Drive (C5).
Directions From Ness Bridge (C3) follow Bridge Street, turn right on to Castle Street, follow this route on to Culduthel Road,

take the fifth right turning on to Drummond Road, then the first or second right on to Glenburn Drive.

STB rating B&B **

MRS Z. MACDONALD
5 Muirfield Gardens, Inverness IV2 4HF
Tel (01463) 238114
Open February to December
Rooms 2 double, 1 twin.
Prices B&B – single, £15–£18; double/twin, £15–£18.
Ver TV in room; tea/coffee facilities; private parking; use of iron.
Location Muirfield Gardens (D5).
Directions From Ness Bridge (C3) follow Bridge Street, turn right on to Castle Street, follow on to Culduthel Road, take the sixth left turning on to Muirfield Road, take the first right turn on to Muirfield Gardens.

STB rating B&B ***

MRS M. MACISAAC
Griais, 1 Wimberley Way, Inverness IV2 3XJ
Tel (01463) 221603
Open All year
Rooms 1 double, 2 twin, 1 en-suite.
Prices B&B – single, £18–£22; double/twin, £18–£20.
Ver TV in lounge; tea/coffee facilities; non-smoking; limited parking.
Directions To Wimberley Way from Ness Bridge (Map 1 – C3) follow Bridge Street, turn right on to Castle Street, take first left on to Old Edinburgh Road, take fifth left on to Annfield Road, drive to the end, then take left turning on to Damfield Road, continue on to Culcabock Road, look out for clubhouse and car park on the right, directly opposite on the left is Wimberley Way.

STB rating B&B ***

MR C. AND MRS J. MACKAY
Glen Fruin, 50 Fairfield Road, Inverness IV3 5QW
Tel (01463) 712623
Open All year
Rooms 1 double, 1 twin, 1 family, 2 en-suite.

Prices B&B – double/twin, £17–£20.

Ver TV in room; tea/coffee facilities; non-smoking; limited parking; pay phone available.

Location Fairfield Road (A3).

Directions From Ness Bridge (C3) follow Young Street and Tomnahurich Street, away from the town centre, take the fourth right turn after the bridge on to Kenneth Street, take the second left turning on to Fairfield Road.

STB rating B&B **

MRS A. MACKENZIE

5 Crown Circus, Inverness IV2 3NH

Tel (01463) 224222

Open All year

Rooms 1 single, 1 double, 1 family, 1 en-suite.

Prices B&B from £17.

Ver Tea/coffee facilities; non-smoking; limited parking; use of iron.

Location Crown Circus (D2).

Directions From Ness Bridge (C3) turn right on to Bank Street, turn right on to Friar's Lane, turn right on to Academy Street, turn left on to Millburn Road, and take a sharp right at Eastgate Shopping Centre, passing under two footbridges, follow on to Crown Road, take a sharp left at the next junction on to Crown Circus.

Comments Enjoy a warm welcome in a family-run B&B in a Victorian villa situated in a residential area. It is five minutes from the town centre, bus and rail stations. Ideal base for touring Loch Ness and the Highlands. No smoking throughout the house.

STB rating B&B ***

MRS A.E. MACKINNON

6 Broadstone Park, Inverness IV2 3LA

Tel (01463) 221506

Open All year

Rooms 1 single, 1 twin, 1 family, 2 en-suite, 1 private facility.

Prices B&B – single, £21–£25; double/twin, £20–£25.

Ver TV in room; tea/coffee facilities; non-smoking; limited parking; pay phone available; use of iron.

Non-ver Vegetarian and special diets available by arrangement;

Gaelic spoken.

Location Broadstone Park (D3).

Directions From Ness Bridge (C3) follow Bridge Street, turn right on to Castle Street, turn left on to Old Edinburgh Road, take fourth right turning on to Southside Road, at next junction turn right on to Kingsmills Road, take the first left turning on to Broadstone Park.

STB rating B&B ***

MRS A.E. MCCLOREY

Bunillidh, 47 Montague Row, Inverness IV3 5DX

Tel (01463) 225079

Open January to December

Rooms 1 single, 1 double, 1 twin, 1 family, 1 en-suite.

Prices B&B – single, £16–£18; double/twin, £18–£20; B&B plus evening meal, £28–£30.

Ver Non-smoking; use of iron; evening meal available.

Location Montague Row (B3).

Directions From Ness Bridge (C3) follow Young Street on to Tomnahurich Street and take the fifth right turning on to Montague Row.

STB rating B&B ***

MRS N.M. MCKINNIE

Furan Cottage, 100 Old Edinburgh Road, Inverness IV2 3HT

Tel (01463) 712094

Open All year

Rooms 1 single, 1 double, 1 family, 1 private facility.

Prices B&B – single, £15–£18; double/twin, £15–£18; B&B plus evening meal, £25–£28.

Ver TV in room; non-smoking; limited parking; use of iron; evening meal by arrangement.

Location Old Edinburgh Road (C3/D4).

Directions From Ness Bridge (C3) follow Bridge Street, turn right on to Castle Street, turn left on to Old Edinburgh Road.

STB rating B&B **

MELNESS GUEST HOUSE

8 Old Edinburgh Road, Inverness IV2 3HF

Tel (01463) 220963   *Fax* (01463) 220963

Open January to December
Rooms 1 double, 1 twin, 1 family en-suite.
Prices B&B from £18.
Location Old Edinburgh Road (C3/D4).
Directions From Ness Bridge (C3) follow Bridge Street, turn right on to Castle Street, turn left on to Old Edinburgh Road.
Comments Melness offers guests a comfortable stay just five minutes from the town centre, rail and bus stations. All rooms have tea/coffee, central heating and colour TVs.
STB rating B&B ***

MRS JOHAN MUIR
Lynwood, 13 Ross Avenue, Inverness IV2 5QJ
Tel (01463) 224758
Open All year
Rooms 1 twin, 1 family.
Prices B&B – single, £13–£16; double/twin, £13–£16.
Ver TV in room; tea/coffee facilities; non-smoking; use of iron.
Non-ver Use of shower and clothes-drying facilities; vegetarian and special diets available by arrangement.
Location Ross Avenue (A3/A2).
Directions From Ness Bridge (C3) follow Young Street and Tomnahurich Street, away from the town centre, take fourth right turning on to Kenneth Street, take second left turning on to Fairfield Road, take third left turning on to Ross Avenue.
STB rating B&B ***

MRS L. ORAM
30 Firthview Road, Muirtown, Inverness IV3 6LZ
Tel (01463) 233853
Open April to October
Rooms 2 twin, 1 en-suite, 1 private facility.
Prices B&B – double/twin, £16–£20.
Ver Tea/coffee facilities; use of lounge; use of iron.
Directions To Firthview Road from Ness Bridge (C3) follow Young Street on to Tomnahurich Street, away from the town centre, take the fourth right turning past the bridge on to Kenneth Street, continue straight forward past the ring road on to Telford Street, cross the Muirtown Bridge, take the second left

turning on to King Brude Road, and take the first right turning on to Firthview Road.

STB rating B&B **

MS M. PHYFER
16 Fairfield Road, Inverness IV3 5QA
Tel (01463) 240309   *Fax* (01463) 240309
Open All year
Rooms 1 single, 1 twin, 1 family, 3 en-suites.
Prices B&B – single, £14–£22; double/twin, £14–£25; B&B plus evening meal, £25.
Ver TV in room; tea/coffee facilities; non-smoking; private parking; evening meal by arrangement; pay phone available; use of iron.
Location Fairfield Road (A3).
Directions From Ness Bridge (C3) follow Young Street on to Tomnahurich Street, away from the town centre, take the fourth right turn on to Kenneth Street, take the second left turn on to Fairfield Road.

STB rating B&B **

PITFARANNE
57 Crown Street, Inverness IV2 3AY
Tel (01463) 239338
Open All year
Rooms 2 double, 2 twin, 1 family, 1 en-suite, 4 private facilities.
Prices B&B – single, £17–£19; double/twin, £16–£18.
Ver TV in room; tea/coffee facilities; non-smoking; private facilities; pay phone available; use of lounge.
Location Crown Street (C3).
Directions From Ness Bridge (C3) follow Bridge Street, turn right on to Castle Street, turn left on to Old Edinburgh Road, take the second left turning on to Mitchell's Lane, drive to the end and turn right on to Argyle Street, turn left up Denny Street and stop at Crown Street.

STB rating B&B **

MRS PRESTON
Advie Lodge, 31 Crown Drive, Inverness IV2 3QQ
Tel (01463) 237247

Open January to December

Rooms 1 single, 1 double, 1 twin, 2 en-suites.

Prices B&B – single, £18–£20; double/twin, £18–£20.

Ver TV in room; tea/coffee facilities; non-smoking; private parking; use of lounge; use of iron.

Location Crown Drive (D2).

Directions From Ness Bridge (C3) turn right down Bank Street, turn right on to Friar's Lane, turn right on to Academy Street, turn left towards the Eastgate Shopping Centre, turn a sharp right passing under two footbridges, follow Crown Road until the first junction and continue on to Crown Drive.

STB rating B&B ***

SEALLADH SONA

3 Whinpark, Canal Road, Muirtown, Inverness IV3 8NQ

Tel (01463) 239209   *Fax* (01463) 239209

E-mail cooksona@aol.com

Open February to November

Rooms 1 double en-suite, 2 twin en-suite.

Prices B&B – £24–£28.

Ver TV in room; tea/coffee facilities; non-smoking; private parking; pay phone available; use of lounge; use of hairdryer and iron.

Directions To Whinpark from Ness Bridge (C3) follow Young Street and Tomnahurich Street, away from the town centre, take the fourth right turn on to Kenneth Street, follow this route up to the ring road, go straight ahead and along Telford Street, cross the Muirtown Bridge, take a left turn on to Canal Road, and take the first right turning to Whinpark.

Comments Comfortable Victorian cottage overlooking canal. Ten minutes from town centre.

STB rating B&B ****

MRS M. SHIELDS

Ardgowan, 45 Fairfield Road, Inverness IV3 5QP

Tel (01463) 236489

Open All year

Rooms 1 twin, 1 double/family, 1 en-suite.

Prices B&B – single from £16.50; double/twin from £16.50.

Ver TV in room; tea/coffee facilities; non-smoking; limited parking.

Non-ver Use of shower; iron and clothes-drying facilities; vegetarian and special diets available by arrangement.

Location Fairfield Road (A2/A3).

Directions From Ness Bridge (C3) follow Young Street on to Tomnahurich Street, away from the town centre, take the fourth right turning after the bridge on to Kenneth Street, take the second left turning on to Fairfield Road.

STB rating B&B **

MRS SINCLAIR

7 Broadstone Avenue, Inverness IV2 3LE

Tel (01463) 225728

Open January to December

Rooms 2 double, 1 family, 3 en-suite.

Prices B&B – single, £20–£25; double/twin, £18–£25.

Ver TV in room; tea/coffee facilities; non-smoking; limited parking; TV in lounge.

Location Broadstone Avenue (D3).

Directions From Ness Bridge (C3) follow Bridge Street, turn right on to Castle Street, turn right on to Old Edinburgh Road, take the fourth left turning on to Southside Road, take a sharp right turn on to Kingsmills Road, take the second left turning on to Broadstone Avenue.

STB rating B&B **

MRS D. SMITH

Lyndon B&B, 50 Telford Street, Inverness IV3 5LE

Tel (01463) 232551

Open All year

Rooms 1 double, 1 twin, 1 family, 2 en-suite, 1 private facility.

Prices B&B – single from £18; double/twin from £15.

Ver TV in room (also satellite TV which can be fed through the TV system in each room); tea/coffee facilities; non-smoking; private parking; pay phone available; use of iron.

Location Telford Street (A2).

Directions From Ness Bridge (C3) follow Young Street and Tomnahurich Street, away from the town centre, take fourth right turning past the bridge on to Kenneth Street, on reaching the ring road drive straight forward on to Telford Street.

STB rating B&B ***

MRS J.M. STEWART
Bridge House, 19 Harris Road, Inverness IV2 3LS
Tel (01463) 714770
Open All year
Rooms 2 single, 1 twin.
Prices B&B – single, £17–£18; double/twin, £17–£18.
Ver TV in room; tea/coffee facilities; private parking; pay phone available; use of lounge; use of iron.
Location Harris Road (E5).
Directions From Ness Bridge (C3) follow Bridge Street, turn right on to Castle Street, turn left on to Old Edinburgh Road, take the sixth turning to the left on to Damfield Road, then take the second turning to the right on to Harris Road.
STB rating B&B **

MRS R.A. STEWART
5 Trafford Avenue, Inverness IV3 5LW
Tel (01463) 240108
Open May to September
Rooms 1 twin, 1 family, 2 en-suite.
Prices B&B – double/twin, £18.
Ver TV in room; tea/coffee facilities; non-smoking; private parking; pay phone available; use of iron.
Directions To Trafford Avenue from Ness Bridge (C3) follow Young Street on to Tomnahurich Street away from town centre, take fourth right turn past the bridge on to Kenneth Street, take second left on to Fairfield Road, take the eighth right turning on to Balnacraig Road, take the first left turning on to Trafford Avenue.
STB rating B&B ***

MRS TAYLOR
Ardentorrie House, 2 Gordon Terrace, Inverness IV2 3HD
Tel (01463) 230090
Open All year
Rooms 1 single, 1 double, 1 family, 3 en-suite.
Prices B&B – single, £16–£20; double/twin, £18–£20.
Ver TV in room; tea/coffee facilities; non-smoking; private parking; pay phone available; use of iron.
Location Gordon Terrace (C3).

Directions From Ness Bridge (C3) follow Bridge Street, take a right turn on to Castle Street, take a sharp left turn on to Gordon Terrace.
STB rating B&B **

TORRIDON GUEST HOUSE
59 Kenneth Street, Inverness IV3 5PZ
Tel (01463) 236449   *Fax* (01463) 236449
E-mail louise@torridon.dial.intermedia.co.uk
Open All year
Rooms 3 family, 2 en-suite, 1 private facility.
Prices B&B – double/twin, £15–£19.
Ver TV in room; tea/coffee facilities; limited parking; pay phone available; use of hairdryer and iron.
Non-ver Use of shower; iron and clothes-drying facilities; packed lunches by arrangement; pets welcome by arrangement; vegetarian and special diets available.
Location Kenneth Street (B2/B3).
Directions From Ness Bridge (C3) follow Young Street on to Tomnahurich Street, away from the town centre, take the fourth right turning past the bridge on to Kenneth Street.
STB rating B&B **

MRS JENNIFER WILSON
Cairnsmore, 41 Charles Street, Inverness IV2 3AH
Tel (01463) 233485
Open All year
Rooms 2 double, 1 twin.
Prices B&B – Double/twin, £15–£18.50.
Ver TV in room; tea/coffee facilities; non-smoking; use of iron.
Non-ver Packed lunches available by arrangement; baby's cot available; vegetarian and special diets by arrangement; use of shower and iron.
Location Charles Street (C3).
Directions From Ness Bridge (C3) follow Bridge Street, turn right on to Castle Street, turn left on to Old Edinburgh Road, take second left turn on to Mitchell's Lane, turn right on to Argyle Street, turn left up Denny Street past Crown Street and Hill Street and reach Charles Street.
STB rating ****

WHITELODGE

WHITELODGE

15 Bishop's Road, Inverness IV3 5SB

Tel (01463) 230693/(01463) 717667 *Fax* (01463) 230693

Open All year

Rooms 1 double (includes four-poster bed), 1 twin, 1 family, 1 single.

Prices B&B from £20–£30.

Ver All rooms with all facilities; non-smoking; private parking.

Location Bishop's Road (B4).

Directions From Ness Bridge (C3) cross the bridge and turn left on to Ness Walk, and continue on to Bishop's Road.

Comments Just ten minutes' walk from the town centre.

STB rating B&B ****

L.H. ZEFFERT

11 Mayfield Road, Inverness IV2 4AE

Tel (01463) 713949

Open All year

Rooms 2 twin, 1 en-suite, 1 private facility.

Prices B&B – single, £18–£20; double/twin, £15–£19.

Ver TV in room; tea/coffee facilities; non-smoking; private parking; use of hairdryer and iron.

Location Mayfield Road (C4).

Directions From Ness Bridge (C3) follow Bridge Street, turn right on to Castle Street, follow on to Culduthel Road, take second left turning on to Mayfield Road.

STB rating B&B **

GUEST HOUSES

ABERFELDY GUEST HOUSE

11 Southside Road, Inverness IV2 3BG

Tel (01463) 231120   *Fax* (01463) 234741

Open All year

Rooms 1 single, 3 double, 2 twin, 3 family, 9 en-suite.

Prices B&B from £19.

Ver TV in room; tea/coffee facilities; non-smoking; private parking; evening meal by arrangement; pay phone available; use of hairdryer, iron and lounge.

Non-ver Packed lunches and vegetarian and special diets by arrangement.

Location Southside Road (C4).

Directions From Ness Bridge (C3) follow Bridge Street, turn right on to Castle Street, continue on to Culduthel Road, take the third left turning on to Southside Road.

Comments A five-minute walk from the town centre and an eight-minute walk from both train and bus station. Ideally situated to take in all that Inverness and the surrounding areas have to offer.

STB rating Guest House ***

ABERMAR GUEST HOUSE

25 Fairfield Road, Inverness IV3 5QD

Tel (01463) 239019

Open All year

Rooms 5 single, 2 double, 2 twin, 2 family, 3 en-suite, 2 private facility.

Prices B&B – single, £17–£18; double/twin, £34–£36 (room only).

Ver TV in room; tea/coffee facilities; limited parking; pay phone available; use of lounge, hairdryer and iron.

Location Fairfield Road (A2/A3).

Directions From Ness Bridge (C3) follow Young Street on to Tomnahurich Street, away from the town centre, take the fourth right turning after the bridge on to Kenneth Street, take the second left turning on to Fairfield Road.

STB rating Guest House *

ACH ALUINN GUEST HOUSE

27 Fairfield Road, Inverness IV3 5QD

Tel (01463) 230127   *Fax* (01463) 230127

Open All year

Rooms 1 single, 2 twin, 2 family, 4 en-suite, 1 private facility.

Prices B&B – single, £20–£25; double/twin, £20–£25.

Ver TV in room with satellite facility; tea/coffee facilities; non-smoking; private parking; use of iron.

Non-ver Packed lunches and vegetarian and special diets by arrangement; use of clothes-drying facilities.

Location Fairfield Road (A2/A3).

Directions From Ness Bridge (C3) follow Young Street on to Tomnahurich Street, away from the town centre, take the fourth right turning on to Kenneth Street, take the second left turning on to Fairfield Road.

STB rating Guest House ***

ARDCONNEL HOUSE

21 Ardconnel Street, Inverness IV2 3EU

Tel (01463) 240455/(01463) 717955 *Fax* (01463) 240455

Open All year

Rooms 1 double, 1 double en-suite, 1 single en-suite, 1 family en-suite, 1 twin private facility.

Prices B&B from £19.

Location Ardconnel Street (C3).

Directions From Ness Bridge (C3) follow Bridge Street, turn right on to Castle Street, take first left turn on to Old Edinburgh Road, take fourth left turning on to Southside Road, follow on to Kingsmills Road, take fourth left turning on to Ardconnel Terrace, follow on to Ardconnel Street.

Comments Five minutes from coach and train stations.

STB rating Guest House ****

ARDMUIR HOUSE HOTEL

16 Ness Bank, Inverness IV2 4SF

Tel (01463) 231151   *Fax* (01463) 231151

Open All year

Rooms 1 single, 5 double, 2 twin, 2 family, 10 en-suite.

Prices B&B – single, £33.50–£36; double/twin, £27.50–£33; B&B plus evening meal, £40.50–£47.

Ver TV in room; tea/coffee facilities; telephone in room; non-smoking; limited parking; use of hairdryer and iron.

Non-ver Use of baby's cot; vegetarian and special diets available; credit/debit cards accepted.

Location Ness Bank (C4).

Directions From Ness Bridge (C3) turn left on to Castle Road running alongside River Ness, take the first right turning to Ness Bank.

Comments Situated beside the River Ness close to the town centre and Ness Islands, it is an ideal base for exploring the Highlands. Brochure and tariff with discounts for stays of three days or more is available from the proprietors, Jean and Tony Gatcombe.

STB rating Guest House ***

ATHOLDENE HOUSE
20 Southside Road, Inverness IV2 3BG
Tel (01463) 233565   *Fax* (01463) 233565
Open All year
Rooms 2 single, 2 double, 4 twin, 1 family, 7 en-suite.
Prices B&B – single, £28–£40; double/twin, £20–£25.
Ver TV in room; tea/coffee facilities; private parking; pay phone available; use of hairdryer and iron.
Non-ver Use of shower; iron and clothes-drying facilities; pets welcome by arrangement; credit/debit cards accepted.
Location Southside Road (C4).
Directions From Ness Bridge (C3) turn right on to Castle Street, follow on to Culduthel Road, take the third left turning on to Southside Road.
Comments Atholdene House is situated in a lovely residential area. Private car parking available.
STB rating Guest House **

AVALON GUEST HOUSE
79 Glenurquhart Road, Inverness IV3 5PB
Tel (01463) 239075
Open February to November
Rooms 2 single, 2 double, 1 twin, 1 family, 5 en-suite, 1 private facility.
Prices B&B – single, £20–£30; double/twin, £20–£26.
Ver TV in room; tea/coffee facilities; non-smoking; private parking; pay phone available.
Non-ver Use of shower and baby's cot; vegetarian and special diets available by arrangement.
Location Glenurquhart Road (A5).
Directions From Ness Bridge (C3) follow Young Street on to Tomnahurich Street, away from the town centre, continue on to Glenurquhart Road.
STB rating Guest House ****

BALLIFEARY HOUSE HOTEL
10 Ballifeary Road, Inverness IV3 5PJ
Tel (01463) 235572   *Fax* (01463) 717583
E-mail ballifhotel@btinternet.com
Website www.ibmpcug.co.uk/-ecs/hotel/ballif/

Open April to October

Rooms 3 double, 2 twin, 5 en-suite.

Prices B&B – single, £40–£55; double/twin, £34–£36; B&B plus evening meal, £53.50–£55.50.

Ver TV in room; tea/coffee facilities; non-smoking; private parking; pay phone available; use of hairdryer and iron.

Non-ver Credit/debit cards accepted.

Location Ballifeary Road (A5/B4/B3).

Directions From Ness Bridge (C3) follow Young Street on to Tomnahurich Street, away from the town centre, continue on to Glenurquhart Road, take the fourth left turning on to Ballifeary Road.

Comments Ballifeary House enjoys an excellent reputation. Ideally situated in a desirable, quiet, residential area, and just ten minutes' picturesque walk to town. All bedrooms have en-suite bathrooms. Home cooking, car park and no-smoking throughout.

STB rating Guest House *****

BORVE HOUSE

9 Old Edinburgh Road, Inverness IV2 3HF

Tel (01463) 234728   *Fax* (01463) 711017

Open All year

Rooms 1 double, 1 twin, 2 family, 4 en-suite.

Prices B&B – single from £22; double/twin from £22.

Ver TV in room; tea/coffee facilities; non-smoking; private parking; pay phone available; use of lounge and iron.

Non-ver Use of shower; packed lunches by arrangement; pets welcome by arrangement; vegetarian and special diets available.

Location Old Edinburgh Road (C3/D4).

Directions From Ness Bridge (C3) follow Bridge Street, turn right on to Castle Street, continue on to Culduthel Road, take first left turning on to Old Edinburgh Road.

Comments Built in 1841, this beautiful Victorian town house has been tastefully refurbished. Only five minutes' walk to River Ness, Castle and the theatre. Courtesy car to and from the station.

STB rating Guest House ***

BREWERS HOUSE BED & BREAKFAST

2 Moray Park, Island Bank Road, Inverness IV2 4SX

Tel (01463) 235557

Open All year

Rooms 1 single, 2 double, 1 twin, 1 family, 5 en-suite.

Prices B&B – single, £18–£20; double/twin, £18–£20.

Ver TV in room; tea/coffee facilities; non-smoking; use of hairdryer and iron.

Location Moray Park (C4).

Directions From Ness Bridge (C3) turn down Castle Road, away from the town centre, follow on to Haugh Road, continue on to Island Bank Road, turn left on to Moray Park opposite River Ness suspension bridge and Cavell Gardens.

Comments Ideally situated overlooking Cavell Gardens and River Ness, proprietors Alistair and Elizabeth assure you of a warm welcome and friendly atmosphere in their 150-year-old house. Only a short stroll along the riverbank from the town centre, Brewers House is an ideal central Highlands location.

STB rating Guest House ***

CEDAR VILLA GUEST HOUSE

33 Kenneth Street, Inverness IV3 5DH

Tel (01463) 230477   *Fax* (01463) 230477

Open All year

Rooms 1 single, 1 double, 1 twin, 3 family, 2 en-suite.

Prices Single, £13–£20; double/twin, £13–£20.

Ver TV in room; tea/coffee facilities; use of iron.

Location Kenneth Street (B2/B3).

Directions From Ness Bridge (C3) follow Young Street on to Tomnahurich Street, away from the town centre, take the fourth right turning on to Kenneth Street.

STB rating Guest House **

CRAIGSIDE LODGE

4 Gordon Terrace, Inverness IV2 3HD

Tel (01463) 231576   *Fax* (01463) 713409

Open All year

Rooms 3 double, 3 twin, 6 en-suite.

Prices B&B – single, £20–£22; double/twin, £19–£22.

Ver TV in room; tea/coffee facilities; non-smoking; private

parking; pay phone available; use of lounge; hairdryer and iron.
Non-ver Use of shower and baby's cot; credit/debit cards accepted.
Location Gordon Terrace (C3).
Directions From Ness Bridge (C3) follow Bridge Street, turn right
on to Castle Street, take the first left turn on to Old Edinburgh
Road, ignore the entry to Gordon Terrace (it is a one-way
street), take the second left turning on to Mitchell's Lane, turn
left on to Argyle Street, turn left on to Gordon Terrace.
STB rating Guest House **

DALMORE GUEST HOUSE
101 Kenneth Street, Inverness IV3 5QQ
Tel (01463) 237224
Open All year
Rooms 2 single, 1 double, 1 twin, 2 family.
Prices B&B – single, £18; double/twin, £15.
Location Kenneth Street (B2/B3).
Directions From Ness Bridge (C3) follow Young Street on to
Tomnahurich Street, away from the town centre, take the
fourth right turning past the bridge on to Kenneth Street.
STB rating Guest House **

EAST DENE
6 Ballifeary Road, Inverness IV3 5PJ
Tel (01463) 232976   *Fax* (01463) 232976
E-mail dgreig@nildram.co.uk
Open All year
Rooms 2 double en-suite, 1 twin en-suite, 1 double private facility.
Prices B&B – double/twin, £22–£28.
Ver TV in room; tea/coffee facilities; non-smoking; private
parking; evening meal available; pay phone available; use of
lounge; hairdryer and iron.
Location Ballifeary Road (A5/B5/B4).
Directions From Ness Bridge (C3) follow Young Street on to
Tomnahurich Street, away from the town centre, continue on
to Glenurquhart Road, take the fourth left turning on to
Ballifeary Road.
STB rating Guest House ***

EDEN HOUSE
8 Ballifeary Road, Inverness IV3 5PJ
Tel (01463) 230278   *Fax* (01463) 230278
Open All year
Rooms 2 double, 2 twin, 1 family, 5 en-suite.
Prices Single, £40–£66; double/twin, £27–£33.
Ver Tea/coffee facilities; non-smoking; private parking; pay phone available; use of lounge and hairdryer.
Non-ver Use of shower and iron; vegetarian and special diets available; credit/debit cards accepted.
Location Ballifeary Road (A5/B5/B4).
Directions From Ness Bridge (C3) follow Young Street on to Tomnahurich Street, away from the town centre, continue on to Glenurquhart Road, take fourth left turning on to Ballifeary Road.
Comments Victorian house, close to theatre, in peaceful setting. Ten-minute walk from the town centre, Eden House is elegantly furnished. Three-day special break for spring and autumn.
STB rating Guest House *****

EDENVIEW
26 Ness Bank, Inverness IV2 4SF
Tel (01463) 234397
Open March to October
Rooms 1 double, 1 twin, 1 family, 2 en-suite, 1 private facility.
Prices B&B – double/twin from £20.
Ver TV in room; non-smoking; private parking; use of lounge; hairdryer and iron.
Location Ness Bank (C4).
Directions From Ness Bridge (C3) turn left at Ness Bridge, follow Castle Road, away from the town centre, take first right turning on to Ness Bank.
STB rating Guest House ***

ESKDALE GUEST HOUSE
41 Greig Street, Inverness IV3 5PX
Tel (01463) 240933   *Fax* (01463) 240933
Open All year
Rooms 1 single, 2 double, 1 twin, 2 family, 3 en-suite.

Prices B&B – single, £20–£22; double/twin, £16–£22; B&B plus evening meal, £28–£34.

Ver TV in room; tea/coffee facilities; non-smoking; private parking; evening meal available; pay phone available; use of lounge and iron.

Non-ver Use of shower and clothes-drying facilities; vegetarian and special diets available.

Location Greig Street (B3).

Directions From Ness Bridge (C3) follow Young Street on to Tomnahurich Street, away from the town centre, take the fourth right turn on to Kenneth Street, take the second right turn on to Greig Street.

Comments Situated in the heart of Inverness, only five minutes from the station. Home cooking, private parking, discounts for stays over three days.

STB rating Guest House ***

FAIRWAYS GUEST HOUSE

72 Telford Road, Inverness IV3 6HN

Tel (01463) 224934   *Fax* (01463) 224934

Open January to December (excluding Christmas and New Year).

Rooms 2 double, 4 twin, 1 family, 3 en-suite.

Prices B&B – double/twin, £14–£20; B&B plus evening meal, £20–£26.

Ver TV in room with satellite facility; tea/coffee facilities; non-smoking; private parking; evening meal; payphone available.

Location Telford Road (A2/A1).

Directions From Ness Bridge (C3) follow Young Street on to Tomnahurich Street, away from the town centre, take fourth turning past the bridge on to Kenneth Street, at ring road follow straight on to Telford Street, take second right turning on to Telford Road. (Note This is a one-way street and can only be accessed from Telford Street.)

STB rating Guest House **

FELSTEAD HOUSE

18 Ness Bank, Inverness IV2 4SF

Tel (01463) 231634   *Fax* (01463) 231634

E-mail jaf@yrl.co.uk

Website www.nwnet.co.uk/jafworld/felstead.htm

Open All year

Ver TV in room; tea/coffee facilities; non-smoking; private parking; pay phone available; use of TV in lounge and hairdryer.

Location Ness Bank (C4).

Directions From Ness Bridge (C3) turn left down Castle Road, turn right on to Ness Bank.

Comments Georgian house overlooking River Ness and close to the town centre and the castle. Colour brochure available.

STB rating Guest House ****

INVERGLEN GUEST HOUSE

7 Abertarff Road, Inverness IV2 3NW

Tel (01463) 237610

Open All year

Rooms 2 double, 1 twin, 2 family, 5 en-suite.

Prices B&B – single, £22–£25; double/twin, £18–£24; B&B plus evening meal, £18–£24.

Location Abertarff Road (D2).

Directions From Ness Bridge (C3) turn right on to Bank Street, turn right on to Friar's Lane, turn right on to Academy Street, turn left at the Eastgate Shopping Centre, take a sharp right turn, passing under two footbridges and continue on to Crown Road, follow on to Crown Drive, take first right turn on to Abertarff Road.

STB rating Guest House ***

IVANHOE GUEST HOUSE

68 Lochalsh Road, Inverness IV3 6HW

Tel (01463) 223020   *Fax* (01463) 223020

Open All year

Rooms 2 single, 1 double, 1 twin, 1 family, 2 en-suite.

Prices B&B – single, £16–£18; double/twin, £17–£18.

Ver TV in room; tea/coffee facilities; non-smoking; pay phone available; use of hairdryer and iron.

Location Lochalsh Road (A2).

Directions From Ness Bridge (C3) follow Young Street on to Tomnahurich Street, away from the town centre, take the fourth right turning past the bridge on to Kenneth Street, take the second left turning on to Fairfield Road, take the fifth right turning on to Lochalsh Road. (Note: this is a one-way street and can only be accessed from Fairfield Road.)

STB rating Guest House **

IVYBANK GUEST HOUSE

28 Old Edinburgh Road, Crown, Inverness IV2 3HJ

Tel (01463) 232796   *Fax* (01463) 232796

Open All year

Rooms 3 double, 1 twin, 1 family, 3 en-suite, 1 private facility.

Prices B&B – single, £25–£28; double/twin, £22.50–£25.

Ver TV in room; tea/coffee facilities; non-smoking; pay phone available; use of lounge; hairdryer and iron.

Non-ver Packed lunches and vegetarian and special diets by arrangement; pets welcome by arrangement; use of shower and clothes-drying facilities.

Location Old Edinburgh Road (C3/D4).

Directions From Ness Bridge (C3) follow Bridge Street, turn right on to Castle Street, take second left turn on to Old Edinburgh Road.

Comments This listed Georgian home is near the town centre, the castle and the River Ness. Original fireplaces, open fires, beamed and panelled hall, mahogany staircase, walled and landscaped garden, security lighting.

STB rating Guest House ****

KINKELL HOUSE

11 Old Edinburgh Road, Inverness IV2 3HF

Tel (01463) 235243   *Fax* (01463) 225255

E-mail clare@kinkell.freeserve.co.uk

Open All year

Rooms 1 single, 2 double, 4 family, 3 en-suite.

Prices B&B – single, £17–£21; double/twin, £17–£26.

Ver TV in lounge; tea/coffee facilities; non-smoking; private parking; pay phone available; use of lounge and iron.

Location Old Edinburgh Road (C3/D4).

Directions From Ness Bridge (C3) follow Bridge Street, turn right on to Castle Street, take first left turn on to Old Edinburgh Road.

Comments Tastefully decorated Victorian family home, five minutes' walk from the town centre. Spacious accommodation.

STB rating Guest House ***

13-15 Ness Bank, Inverness IV2 4SF
Tel (01463) 233874   *Fax* (01463) 711600
Open All year
Rooms 4 single, 3 double, 6 twin, 3 family, 9 en-suite, 3 private facility.
Prices B&B – single, £20–£30; double/twin, £20–£30.
Ver TV in room; tea/coffee facilities; limited parking; use of TV in lounge.
Non-ver Use of shower; iron and clothes-drying facilities; use of baby's cot; vegetarian and special diets by arrangement.
Location Ness Bank (C4).
Directions From Ness Bridge (C3) take left turn down Castle Road, take right turn on to Ness Bank.
Comments Situated on the bank of the River Ness in a peaceful area close to the town centre, theatre, castle and Ness Islands.
STB rating Guest House *

MRS A. MACKENZIE
21 Ardconnel Street, Inverness IV2 3EU
Tel (01463) 240455/ 717955   *Fax* (01463) 240455
Open All year
Rooms 1 single, 2 double, 1 twin, 2 family, 3 en-suite, 1 private facility.
Prices B&B – single, £21–£22; double/twin, £19–£22.
Ver TV in room; tea/coffee facilities; non-smoking; use of lounge and iron.
Location Ardconnel Street (C3).
Directions From Ness Bridge (C3) follow Bridge Street, turn right on to Castle Street, turn left on to Old Edinburgh Road, take fourth left turning on to Southside Road, follow on to Kingsmills Road, take fourth left turning on to Ardconnel Terrace, follow on to Ardconnel Street.
STB rating Guest House ****

MACRAE GUEST HOUSE
24 Ness Bank, Inverness IV2 4SF
Tel (01463) 243658
Open All year
Rooms 1 double, 2 twin, 2 en-suite, 1 private facility.

Prices B&B from £20–£24.

Ver TV in room; tea/coffee facilities; non-smoking; private parking; use of lounge; hairdryer and iron.

Location Ness Bank (C4).

Directions From Ness Bridge (C3) take a left turn on to Castle Road, take a right turn on to Ness Bank.

STB rating Guest House ***

MARDON GUEST HOUSE

37 Kenneth Street, Inverness IV3 5DN

Tel (01463) 231005

Open All year

Rooms 3 double, 2 twin, 1 family, 3 en-suite.

Prices B&B – single, £15–£21; double/twin, £14–£20.

Ver TV in room; tea/coffee facilities; limited parking; pay phone available; use of iron.

Non-ver Packed lunches available by arrangement; pets welcome by arrangement.

Location Kenneth Street (B2/B3).

Directions From Ness Bridge (C3) follow Young Street on to Tomnahurich Street, away from town centre, take fourth right turning past the bridge on to Kenneth Street.

STB rating Guest House **

MOYNESS HOUSE HOTEL

6 Bruce Gardens, Inverness IV3 5EN

Tel (01463) 233836   *Fax* (01463) 233836

E-mail kayjonesmoyness@msn.com

Website www.freespace.virgin.net/richard.jones18/

Open All year

Rooms 1 single, 4 double, 2 twin, 7 en-suite.

Prices B&B – single, £28–£34; double/twin, £28–£34; B&B plus evening meal, £46.50–£52.50.

Ver TV in room; tea/coffee facilities; private parking; evening meal available; restricted liquor licence; pay phone available; use of lounge; hairdryer and iron.

Non-ver Use of baby's cot; pets welcome by arrangement; vegetarian and special diets available; credit/debit cards accepted.

Location Bruce Gardens (A4).

INVERNESS CASTLE

ACADEMY STREET, INVERNESS

1   2   3

Playing Fields

Millburn Academy

Youth Hostel (new)

Scout Hall

Crown

Crown Primary Sch

Inverness College

Site of Castle

Bowling Green

HARBOUR ROAD

SEAFIELD RD

Bus Depot

Government Offices

Fire Station

LONGMAN ROAD

Inverness College of Further & Higher Education

BURNETT ROAD

WALKER PL

HARBOUR ROAD

SHORE STREET RD

LOTLAND

Inverness Station

Car Pk

Chapel Yard

CHAPEL ST

ACADEMY ST

BANK

FRIARS

DOUGLAS ROW

Methodist

Murtown Green

Bridge

Waterloo

Huntly Church

INNES ST

CRAN ST

HUNTLY PL

KENNETH STREET

A82

Bishops Primary Sch

Playing Fields

WELLS ST

TELFORD STREET

LOCHALSH ROAD

KESSOCK RD

Football Ground

Merkinch Primary Sch

Merkinch Recreation Ground

Reformed Baptist Ch

Merkinch

INDIA ST

DUNABAN RD

St Michaels Episcopal Church

CAMERON RD

BENULA

CLIFFORD TERR

MONTAGU ROW

PLANEFIELD ROAD

RANGEMORE RD

HARROWDEN RD

CARSE RD

ROSS AVENUE

ARDDALE AVE

GLEBE ST

MIDMILLS

CROWN DRIVE

CROWN ROAD

VICTORIA DRIVE

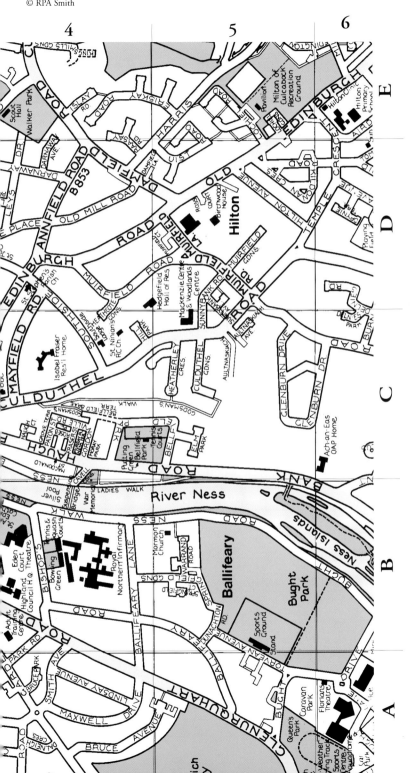

URQUHART CASTLE

FORT AUGUSTUS ABBEY, FORMERLY THE HOME OF THE
BENEDICTINE MONKS, SEVERAL OF WHOM HAVE SEEN NESSIE

THE OFFICIAL LOCH NESS MONSTER EXHIBITION CENTRE,
DRUMNADROCHIT

THE JETTY AT FORT AUGUSTUS, SCENE OF MANY NESSIE
SIGHTINGS

NATURE TRAIL AT INVERFARIGAIG

THE ROUTE TO THE FALLS OF FOYERS

STEVE FELTHAM GETS READY TO SCAN THE SURFACE FOR ANY
SIGN OF MOVEMENT (PHOTOGRAPH © STEVE FELTHAM)

NESSIE WELCOMES VISITORS TO THE CALEDONIAN CANAL AT
FORT AUGUSTUS

THE VILLAGE OF FOYERS

MONSTER ACTIVITIES AT THE GREAT GLEN WATER PARK
(PHOTOGRAPH © MONSTER ACTIVITIES)

Directions From Ness Bridge (C3) follow Young Street on to Tomnahurich Street, away from the town centre, as it turns on to Glenurquhart Road, take first right turning on to Bruce Gardens.

Comments A fine Victorian villa, sympathetically restored, with elegant decoration and furnishings enhancing the many beautiful original features. The bedrooms have en-suite bathrooms. With a pretty garden and ample parking, the hotel is in a quiet area near the town centre, theatre and lovely river walks.

STB rating Guest House *****

NESS BANK HOUSE

7 Ness Bank, Inverness IV2 4SF
Tel (01463) 232939   *Fax* (01463) 232939
Open February to November
Rooms 3 double, 1 twin, 1 family, 2 en-suite, 1 private facility.
Prices B&B – double/twin, £18–£24.
Ver TV in room; tea/coffee facilities; non-smoking; use of iron.
Location Ness Bank (C4).
Directions From Ness Bridge (C3) take left turn down Castle Road, take first right turn on to Ness Bank.
STB rating Guest House ***

OAKFIELD GUEST HOUSE

1 Darnaway Road, Inverness IV2 3LF
Tel (01463) 237926   *Fax* (01463) 718098
E-mail oak@btinternet.com
Website www.members.aol.com/oakfield1/index.htm
Open All year except Christmas and New Year.
Ver TV in room; tea/coffee facilities; non-smoking; private parking; evening meal available; pay phone available; use of lounge; hairdryer and iron.
Non-ver Packed lunches by arrangement; use of shower; credit/debit cards accepted.
Location Darnaway Road (D4/D3).
Directions From Ness Bridge (C3) follow Bridge Street, turn right on to Castle Street, turn left on to Old Edinburgh Road, take the fourth left turning on to Annfield Road, take second left turning on to Darnaway Road.

Comments Oakfield is attractively situated in its own grounds in a quiet residential area close to golf course and local park. The town centre is within easy walking distance and there are many fine restaurants and pubs nearby. Alf and Helen Mackintosh look forward to welcoming you to Oakfield.

STB rating Guest House **

THE OLD RECTORY
9 Southside Road, Inverness IV2 3BG
Tel (01463) 220969
Open All year (except Christmas and New Year).
Rooms 2 double, 2 twin, 4 en-suite.
Prices B&B – single, £20–£25; double/twin, £20–£22.
Ver TV in room; tea/coffee facilities; non-smoking; private parking; pay phone available; use of TV in lounge; hairdryer and iron.
Non-ver Packed lunches available by arrangement; vegetarian and special diets available; credit/debit cards accepted.
Location Southside Road (C4).
Directions From Ness Bridge (C3) follow Bridge Street, turn right on to Castle Street, follow on to Culduthel Road, take third left turning on to Southside Road.
Comments This Victorian house has been tastefully upgraded and decorated. All rooms are en-suite. Only five minutes' walk to town centre and eight minutes' walk to train and bus stations. Private parking is guaranteed. Non-smoking policy.
STB rating Guest House ****

THE OLD ROYAL GUEST HOUSE
10 Union Street, Inverness IV7 7PL
Tel (01463) 230551   *Fax* (01463) 711916
Open All year
Rooms 2 single, 3 double, 3 twin, 2 family, 5 en-suite.
Prices B&B – single, £22–£25; double/twin, £20–£28.
Ver TV in room; tea/coffee facilities; pay phone available; use of lounge and iron.
Non-ver Packed lunches by arrangement; vegetarian and special diets available by arrangement; use of shower and clothes-drying facilities; credit/debit cards accepted.
Location Union Street (C2).

Comments Opposite the railway station. Town centre location ideal for travellers. Twenty-four-hour access.

STB rating Guest House **

PINE GUEST HOUSE

60 Telford Road, Inverness IV3 5LE

Tel (01463) 233032

Open All year

Rooms 3 single, 3 family, 3 en-suite.

Prices B&B – single, £18–£20; double/twin, £18–£22; B&B plus evening meal, £28–£30.

Ver TV in room; tea/coffee facilities; non-smoking; private parking; evening meal available; pay phone available; use of TV in lounge; use of iron.

Non-ver Use of shower; vegetarian and special diets available.

Location Telford Street (A2).

Directions From Ness Bridge (C3) follow Young Street on to Tomnahurich Street, away from the town centre, take fourth right turning on to Kenneth Street, on reaching the ring road go straight forward on to Telford Street.

STB rating Guest House ***

ROSNEATH GUEST HOUSE

39 Greig Street, Inverness IV3 5PX

Tel (01463) 220201   *Fax* (01463) 220201

Open All year

Rooms 2 double, 1 twin, 3 family, 5 en-suite, 1 private facility.

Prices B&B – single, £20–£25; double/twin, £18–£20.

Ver TV in room; tea/coffee facilities; non-smoking; private parking; pay phone available; use of hairdryer and iron.

Non-ver Packed lunches by arrangement; use of shower and baby's cot; vegetarian and special diets by arrangement; credit/debit cards accepted.

Location Greig Street (B3).

Directions From Ness Bridge (C3) follow Young Street on to Tomnahurich Street, away from the town centre, take the fourth right turning on to Kenneth Street, take the third right turning on to Greig Street.

STB rating Guest House ***

7 Midmills Road, Inverness IV2 3NZ
Tel (01463) 225732
Open All year
Rooms 2 double, 1 twin, 3 en-suite.
Prices B&B – single, £20–£40; double/twin, £18–£22.
Ver TV in room; tea/coffee facilities; non-smoking; private parking; pay phone available; use of iron.
Location Midmills Road (D3).
Directions From Ness Bridge (C3) follow Bridge Street, turn right on to Castle Street, take the first left turn on to Old Edinburgh Road, take the fourth right turn on to Southside Road, follow on to Kingsmills Road, then take the second right turning on to Midmills Road.
STB rating Guest House ***

RYEFORD
21 Ardconnel Terrace, Inverness IV2 3AE
Tel (01463) 242871   *Fax* (01463) 242871
Open All year
Rooms 1 single, 1 twin, 2 family, 2 en-suite.
Prices B&B – single, £18–£21; double/twin, £18–£21.
Ver TV in room; tea/coffee facilities; non-smoking; pay phone available; use of TV in lounge; hairdryer and iron.
Location Ardconnel Terrace (C3).
Directions From Ness Bridge (C3) follow Bridge Street, turn right on to Castle Street, take the first left on to Old Edinburgh Road, take the fourth right turn on to Southside Road, follow on to Kingsmills Road, take the fourth left turning on to Ardconnel Terrace.
Comments Situated within minutes of the town centre, bus and train stations, and with open views. A friendly welcome awaits you and your comfort is assured. Early breakfast available.
STB rating Guest House ***

ST ANN'S HOUSE
37 Harrowden Road, Inverness IV3 5QN
Tel (01463) 236157   *Fax* (01463) 236157
E-mail stannshous@aol.com
Website www.hotelinverness.co.uk

Open February to October

Rooms 1 single, 2 double, 2 twin, 1 family, 5 en-suite, 1 private facility.

Prices B&B – single, £20–£25; double/twin, £20–£22.

Ver TV in room; tea/coffee facilities; non-smoking; limited parking; use of TV in lounge; hairdryer and iron.

Non-ver Packed lunches by arrangement; use of baby's cot; vegetarian and special diets by arrangement; restricted liquor licence.

Location Harrowden Road (A2).

Directions From Ness Bridge (C3) follow Young Street on to Tomnahurich Street, away from the town centre, take the fourth right turn after the bridge on to Kenneth Street, take the second left turning on to Fairfield Road, take the fourth right tuning on to Harrowden Road.

STB rating Guest House ***

STRATHMHOR GUEST HOUSE

99 Kenneth Street, Inverness IV3 5QQ

Tel (01463) 235397

Open All year

Rooms 1 single, 2 double, 2 family, 3 en-suite, 1 private facility.

Prices B&B – single, £16–£20; double/twin, £14–£17.50.

Ver TV in lounge; tea/coffee facilities; private parking; use of iron.

Location Kenneth Street (B2/B3).

Directions From Ness Bridge (C3) follow Young Street on to Tomnahurich Street, away from the town centre, take the fourth right turning after the bridge on to Kenneth Street.

STB rating Guest House **

TALISKER GUEST HOUSE

25 Ness Bank, Inverness IV2 4SF

Tel (01463) 236221   *Fax* (01463) 234173

E-mail 106735.2241@compuserve.com

Open All year

Rooms 1 single, 1 double, 2 twin, 2 family, 4 en-suite.

Prices B&B – single, £24–£28; double/twin, £22–£26.

Ver TV in room; tea/coffee facilities; non-smoking; private parking; pay phone available; use of hairdryer and iron.

Non-ver Packed lunches by arrangement; vegetarian and special diets by arrangement; credit/debit cards accepted; use of shower and iron.

Location Ness Bank (C4).

Directions From Ness Bridge (C3) take a left turn on to Castle Road, take the first right turn on to Ness Bank.

STB rating Guest House ***

TRAFFORD BANK

96 Fairfield Road, Inverness IV3 5LL

Tel (01463) 241414

E-mail traff@pop.call.co.uk

Website www./ibmcug.co.uk-cs/guest/trafford/trafford.html

Open All year

Rooms 5 double, 3 twin, 2 family, 5 en-suite.

Prices B&B – single, £40–£60; double/twin, £27.50–£35; B&B plus evening meal, £47.50–£55.

Ver TV in room; tea/coffee facilities; non-smoking; private parking; evening meal available; pay phone available; use of lounge; hairdryer and iron.

Non-ver Vegetarian and special diets by arrangement; use of shower; iron and baby's cot; credit/debit cards accepted.

Location Fairfield Road (A2/A3).

Directions From Ness Bridge (C3) follow Young Street on to Tomnahurich Street, away from the town centre, take the fourth right turning after the bridge on to Kenneth Street, take the second left turning on to Fairfield Road.

STB rating Guest House ***

WHINPARK HOTEL INVERNESS

17 Ardross Street, Inverness IV3 5NS

Tel (01463) 232549   *Fax* (01463) 232549

Open All year

Ver TV in room; tea/coffee facilities; non-smoking; pay phone available; restricted liquor licence; use of TV in lounge; hairdryer and iron.

Non-ver Vegetarian and special diets available; use of baby's cot; credit/debit cards accepted.

Location Ardross Street (B3).

Directions From Ness Bridge (C3) follow Young Street on to Tomnahurich Street, away from the town centre, take the first left turn after Ardross Place on to Ardross Street.

Comments Centrally situated with a high standard of accommodation, within walking distance of the town centre, Eden Court, Cathedral and River Ness. Torvean golf course nearby. All rooms en-suite. Personal, friendly service and warm welcome.

STB rating Guest House ***

WINMAR GUEST HOUSE
78 Kenneth Street, Inverness IV3 5QG

Tel (01463) 239328   *Fax* (01463) 239328

Open All year

Rooms 2 single, 2 double, 2 twin, 1 family, 5 en-suite.

Prices B&B – single, £13–£21; double/twin, £13–£21.

Ver TV in room; tea/coffee facilities; non-smoking; limited parking; pay phone available; use of hairdryer and iron.

Location Kenneth Street (B2/B3).

Directions From Ness Bridge (C3) follow Young Street on to Tomnahurich Street, away from the town centre, take the fourth right turning past the bridge on to Kenneth Street.

STB rating Guest House **

HOTELS
BRAE NESS HOTEL
Ness Bank, Inverness IV2 4SF

Tel (01463) 712266   *Fax* (01463) 231732

Open April to October

Rooms 1 single, 3 double, 4 twin, 2 family, 9 en-suite, 1 private facility.

Prices B&B – single, £30–£37; double/twin, £26–£33; B&B plus evening meal, £41–£51.

Ver TV in room; tea/coffee facilities; non-smoking; private parking.

Non-ver Use of shower, iron and baby's cot; vegetarian and special diets available.

Location Ness Bank (C4).

Directions From Ness Bridge (C3) turn left on to Castle Road, take the first right turning on to Ness Bank.

Comments An 1830 Georgian residence beside the River Ness, five minutes' walk from the town centre, the ten distinctive bedrooms (seven non-smoking) each have private facilities. For dinner and breakfast home cooking is served using only the best quality fresh produce.

STB rating Hotel ***

CHIEFTAIN HOTEL

2 Millburn Road, Inverness IV2 3PS

Tel (01463) 232241

Open All year

Rooms 3 double, 7 twin, 3 family, 13 en-suite.

Prices B&B – double/twin, £25–£30.

Ver TV in room with satellite facility; tea/coffee facilities; telephone in room; private parking; evening meal available.

Location Millburn Road (C4).

Directions From Ness Bridge (C3) turn right on to Bank Street, turn right on to Friar's Lane, turn right on to Academy Street, turn left on to Millburn Road.

STB rating Hotel **

COLUMBA HOTEL

Ness Walk, Inverness IV3 5NE

Tel (01463) 231391   *Fax* (01463) 715526

Open All year

Rooms 18 single, 18 double, 50 twin, 86 en-suite.

Prices B&B – single, £25–£45; double/twin, £25–£45; B&B plus evening meal, £30–£50.

Ver TV in room with satellite facility; tea/coffee facilities; non-smoking; telephone in room; evening meal available.

Location Ness Walk (C3).

Directions From Ness Bridge (C3) cross Ness Bridge, away from the town centre, and take the first left turn on to Ness Walk.

STB rating Hotel *

CRAIGMONIE HOTEL

9 Annfield Road, Inverness IV2 3HX

Tel (01463) 231649   *Fax* (01463) 233720

E-mail infro@craigmonie.com

Open All year

Rooms 4 single, 14 double, 14 twin, 3 family, 35 en-suite.

Prices B&B – single, £68–£74; double/twin, £86–£110.

Ver TV in room including satellite facility; tea/coffee facilities; telephone in room; private parking; evening meal available; use of hairdryer; indoor swimming pool; sauna; jacuzzi; gym; room service; laundry service; porterage.

Non-ver Packed lunches by arrangement; vegetarian and special diets available; use of shower, baby's cot, iron and clothes-drying facilities; credit/debit cards accepted.

Location Annfield Road (D4).

Directions From Ness Bridge (C3) follow Bridge Street, turn right on to Castle Street, turn left on to Old Edinburgh Road, take the fifth left turning on to Annfield Road.

STB rating Hotel ***

CROWN HOTEL

19 Ardconnel Street, Inverness IV2 3EU

Tel (01463) 231135   *Fax* (01463) 231135

Open All year

Rooms 2 single, 1 double, 1 twin, 2 family, 3 en-suite.

Prices B&B – single, £16–£22; double/twin, £17–£19.

Ver TV in room; non-smoking; TV in lounge; pay phone available; use of iron.

Location Ardconnel Street (C3).

Directions From Ness Bridge (C3) follow Bridge Street, turn right on to Castle Street, take first left turn on to Old Edinburgh Road, take third left turning on to Southside Road, continue on to Kingsmills Road, take fourth left turn on to Ardconnel Terrace, continue on to Ardconnel Street.

STB rating Guest House **

CROWN COURT HOTEL

25 Southside Road, Inverness IV2 3BG

Tel (01463) 234816   *Fax* (01463) 714900

Open All year

Rooms 4 double, 1 twin, 1 family, 8 en-suite.

Prices B&B – single, £49.50–£55; double/twin, £39–£47; B&B plus evening meal, £55–£63.

Ver TV in room including satellite facility; tea/coffee facilities; non-smoking; private parking; telephone in room; evening meal available; use of hairdryer; laundry service, porterage.

Location Southside Road (C4).

Directions From Ness Bridge (C3) follow Bridge Street, turn right
on to Castle Street, follow on to Culduthel Road, take the third
right turning on to Southside Road.
STB rating Hotel ****

CUCHULLIN LODGE HOTEL
43 Culduthel Road, Inverness IV2 4HQ
Tel (01463) 231945   *Fax* (01463) 231613
Open March to October
Rooms 3 single, 3 double, 4 twin, 2 family, 11 en-suite.
Prices B&B – double/twin, £35–£42.
Ver TV in room; tea/coffee facilities; private parking; evening meal
available; use of hairdryer.
Non-ver Use of shower for non-en-suite.
Location Culduthel Road (C4).
Directions From Ness Bridge (C3) follow Bridge Street, turn right
on to Castle Street, follow on to Culduthel Road.
STB rating Hotel ****

CULDUTHEL LODGE
14 Culduthel Road, Inverness IV2 4AG
Tel (01463) 240089   *Fax* (01463) 240089
E-mail culduthel@globalnet.co.uk
Open All year
Rooms 1 single, 8 double, 2 twin, 1 family, 12 en-suite.
Prices B&B – single, £45; double/twin, £40–£47; B&B plus
evening meal, £58–£64.
Location Culduthel Road (C4).
Directions From Ness Bridge (C3) follow Bridge Street, turn right
on to Castle Street, follow on to Culduthel Road.
Comments Enjoy relaxed, attentive service. Furnished and
decorated to the highest standard with great attention to detail
and comfort. Daily changing menu of imaginative cooking.
Guest rooms have en-suite facilities, TV, hospitality tray, CD,
flowers, fruit and sherry.
STB rating Hotel ****

Church Street, Inverness IV1 1EN

Tel (01463) 232531   *Fax* (01463) 236541

Open All year

Rooms 6 single, 10 double, 10 twin, 3 family, 23 en-suite, 3 private facility.

Prices B&B – single, £30–£42; double/twin, £30–£40.

Ver TV in room; tea/coffee facilities; telephone in room; non-smoking; evening meal available; laundry service.

Location Church Street (C3).

Directions From Ness Bridge (C3) turn right on to Bank Street, turn right on to Friar's Lane, take the first right turn on to Church Street.

STB rating Hotel **

GLEN MOHR HOTEL AND RESTAURANT

9-12 Ness Bank, Inverness IV2 4SG

Tel (01463) 234308   *Fax* (01463) 713170

Open All year

Rooms 6 single, 7 double, 12 twin, 2 family, 27 en-suite.

Prices B&B – single, £55–£69; double/twin, £37.50–£76; B&B plus evening meal, £57.50.

Ver TV in room; tea/coffee facilities; non-smoking; private parking; evening meal available; room service; porterage; laundry service available; use of hairdryer.

Non-ver Vegetarian meals by arrangement; credit/debit cards accepted.

Location Ness Bank (C4).

Directions From Ness Bridge (C3) turn left on to Castle Road, take the first right turn on to Ness Bank.

Comments Beautifully and quietly situated in central spot on the River Ness. Rooms include standard, executive, four-posters and one suite. Car park. Scottish and ethnic cuisine of renown in two quite different restaurants. Well known for friendly, attentive service. Ideal base for golf, tours, fishing and shooting, shopping and other leisure pursuits. Entertainment some evenings.

STB rating Hotel ***

20 Ness Bank, Inverness IV2 4SF

Tel (01463) 223777   *Fax* (01463) 712378

Open All year

Rooms 2 single, 11 double, 1 twin, 1 family, 15 en-suite.

Prices B&B – single, £65–£95; double/twin, £48–£65; B&B plus evening meal, £70–£90.

Ver TV in room with satellite facility; tea/coffee facilities; private parking; telephone in room; evening meal available; use of hairdryer; room service; laundry service; porterage.

Location Ness Bank (C4).

Directions From Ness Bridge (C3) turn left at the bridge on to Castle Road, take the first right turning on to Ness Bank.

STB rating Hotel ****

Ness Bank, Inverness IV2 4SF

Tel (01463) 233065   *Fax* (01463) 241075

Open All year

Rooms 3 single, 10 double, 10 twin, 2 family, 25 en-suite.

Prices B&B – single, £30–£45; double/twin, £28–£45; B&B plus evening meal, £40–£50.

Ver TV in room; tea/coffee facilities; non-smoking; private parking; evening meal available; laundry service; porterage.

Location Ness Bank (C4).

Directions From Ness Bridge (C3) turn left on to Castle Road, take the first right turning on to Ness Bank.

STB rating Hotel **

Kingsmills Road, Inverness IV2 3JU

Tel (01463) 235877   *Fax* (01463) 715749

E-mail heathmount@cali.co.uk

Open All year

Rooms 2 double, 3 twin, 2 family, 7 en-suite.

Prices B&B – single, £42.50; double/twin, £28.75 (£57.50 room rate).

Ver TV in room; tea/coffee facilities; telephone in room; private parking; evening meal available; use of hairdryer.

Non-ver Vegetarian and special diets available; pets welcome by arrangement; use of shower and baby's cot; credit/debit cards accepted.

Location Kingsmills Road (D3).

Directions From Ness Bridge (C3) follow Bridge Street, turn right on to Castle Street, turn left on to Old Edinburgh Road, take the fourth right turning on to Southside Road, continue on to Kingsmills Road.

Comments The Heathmount is a Highland inn dating back to 1868. Situated close to the town centre. All rooms en-suite. Smoking and non-smoking restaurants offering a wide range of home cooking. The bars stock a range of cask ales and malt whiskies.

STB rating Hotel **

THE INVERNESS THISTLE HOTEL

Millburn Road, Inverness IV2 3TR

Tel (01463) 239666   *Fax* (01463) 711145

Open All year

Rooms 22 single, 37 double, 47 twin, 12 family, 118 en-suite.

Prices B&B – single, £88–£105; double/twin, £108–£130 (room only); B&B plus evening meal, £57–£150.

Ver TV in room with satellite facility; tea/coffee facilities; telephone in room; non-smoking; private parking; evening meal available; porterage; room service; laundry service; use of hairdryer.

Location Millburn Road (D4).

Directions From Ness Bridge (C3) turn right on to Bank Street, turn right on to Friar's Lane, turn right on to Academy Street, turn left on to Millburn Road.

STB rating Hotel ***

JARVIS CALEDONIAN HOTEL

Church Street, Inverness IV1 1DX

Tel (01463) 235181   *Fax* (01463) 711206

Open All year

Rooms 28 single, 8 double, 55 twin, 15 family, 106 en-suite.

Prices B&B – single, £69–£109; double/twin, £40–£75; B&B plus evening meal, £76–£120.

Ver TV in room with satellite facility; tea/coffee facilities; telephone in room; private parking; evening meal available;

indoor swimming pool; room service; laundry service; porterage; use of hairdryer.

Location Church Street (C3).

Directions From Ness Bridge (C3) turn right on to Bank Street, turn right on to Friar's Lane, take the first right turn on to Church Street.

STB rating Hotel ***

KINGSMILLS HOTEL

Culcabock Road, Inverness IV2 3LP

Tel (01463) 237166   *Fax* (01463) 225208

Open All year

Ver TV in room with satellite facility; tea/coffee facilities; telephone in room; private parking; evening meal available; indoor swimming pool; leisure facilities; room service, porterage; laundry service; use of hairdryer.

Non-ver Vegetarian and special diets available; use of baby's cot; pets welcome by arrangement; credit/debit cards accepted.

Directions From Ness Bridge (C3) follow Bridge Street, turn right on to Castle Street, turn left on to Old Edinburgh Road, take the fifth left turning on to Annfield Road (where the road forks) and drive to the end of the road, turn left on to Damfield Road, then follow on to Culcabock Road.

Comments Situated one mile from Inverness town centre and close to famous historic places such as Culloden, Loch Ness, Urquhart Castle and Fort George, the Kingsmills has plenty to offer. Spacious bedrooms all with satellite TV and mini-bars. Leisure club also.

STB rating Hotel ****

LOCHARDIL HOUSE HOTEL

Stratherrick Road, Inverness IV2 4LF

Tel (01463) 235995   *Fax* (01463) 713394

Open All year

Rooms 3 single, 7 double, 2 twin, 12 en-suite.

Prices B&B – single, £60–£70; double/twin, £40–£50; B&B plus evening meal, £70–£75.

Ver TV in room with satellite facility; tea/coffee facilities; telephone in room; limited parking; evening meal available; room service; laundry service; porterage; use of hairdryer.

Directions From Ness Bridge (C3) to Stratherrick Road follow Bridge Street, turn right on to Castle Street, follow on to Culduthel Road, take the fifth right turning on to Drummond Road, take the third right turning on to Merlewood Road, follow on to Stratherrick Road.

STB rating Hotel ****

LOCH NESS HOUSE HOTEL

Glenurquhart Road, Inverness IV3 6JL
Tel (01463) 239327
Open All year
Rooms 2 single, 10 double, 5 twin, 5 family, 22 en-suite.
Prices B&B – single, £40–£60; double/twin, £25–£50; B&B plus evening meal, £55–£65.
Ver TV in room with satellite facility; tea/coffee facilities; telephone in room; private parking; evening meal available; room service; laundry service; use of hairdryer.
Non-ver Use of shower and baby's cot; credit/debit cards accepted.
Location Glenurquhart Road (A5).
Directions From Ness Bridge (C3) follow Young Street on to Tomnahurich Street, continue on to Glenurquhart Road.
Comments Situated beside Torvean golf course and the Caledonian Canal, this is a friendly family-run hotel. Restaurant services fresh seafood and Scottish cuisine. Copper Kettle pub, oyster bar. Excellent bar meals. A warm welcome is ensured.
STB rating Hotel ***

MACDOUGALL CLANSMAN HOTEL

103 Church Street, Inverness IV1 1ES
Tel (01463) 713702   *Fax* (01463) 713702
Open All year
Rooms 2 single, 4 double, 4 twin, 5 family, 13 en-suite, 2 private facility.
Prices B&B – single, £25–£31; double/twin, £21–£27.
Ver TV in room; tea/coffee facilities; limited parking; evening meal available; porterage; laundry service.
Non-ver Packed lunches by arrangement; pets welcome by arrangement; use of iron and clothes-drying facilities.
Location Church Street (C2).
Directions From Ness Bridge (C3) turn right on to Bank Street,

turn right on to Friar's Lane, take first right on to Church Street.

Comments Family-run hotel in convenient town centre location less than five minutes' walk from bus and railway stations. All rooms en-suite or with private facilities. Private parking on request. Residential licence. French, German and Spanish spoken.

STB rating Hotel *

MORAY PARK HOTEL

Island Bank Road, Inverness IV2 4SX

Tel (01463) 233528   *Fax* (01463) 233528

Open All year

Rooms 3 double, 2 twin, 1 family, 6 en-suite.

Prices B&B – single, £28–£42; double/twin, £22–£34; B&B plus evening meal, £36–£56.

Ver TV in room; tea/coffee facilities; private parking; evening meal available; laundry service.

Non-ver Packed lunches by arrangement; credit/debit cards accepted; use of baby's cot, iron and clothes-drying facilities.

Directions From Ness Bridge (C3) to Island Bank Road turn left on to Castle Road, follow on to Haugh Road, follow on to Island Bank Road.

Comments This family-run hotel overlooks Cavell Gardens and the River Ness, yet is only minutes from the town centre. It offers comfortable rooms, fine food and drink, and friendly service. Private parking. European languages.

STB rating Hotel **

PALACE HOTEL AND LEISURE CLUB

Ness Walk, Inverness IV3 5NE

Tel (01463) 223243   *Fax* (01463) 236865

E-mail sales@miltonhotels.com

Website www.miltonhotels.com

Open All year

Rooms 9 single, 20 double, 49 twin, 13 family, all en-suite or private facility.

Prices B&B – single, £74–£104; double/twin, £29.50–£61; B&B plus evening meal, £42–£73.50.

Ver TV in room; tea/coffee facilities; telephone in room; limited parking; evening meal available; room service; indoor swimming pool; leisure facilities; laundry service; porterage.

Location Ness Walk (C3).

Directions From Ness Bridge (C3) cross Ness Bridge, away from town centre, take the first left turning on to Ness Walk.

STB rating Hotel ***

REDCLIFFE HOTEL

1 Gordon Terrace, Inverness IV2 3HD

Tel (01463) 232767   *Fax* (01463) 712279

Open All year

Rooms 3 single, 5 double, 1 twin, 1 family, 7 en-suite.

Prices B&B – single, £20–£30; double/twin, £18–£25; B&B plus evening meal, £27–£35.

Ver TV in room; tea/coffee facilities; telephone in room; limited parking; evening meal available; laundry service; use of hairdryer.

Location Gordon Terrace (C3).

Directions From Ness Bridge (C3) follow Bridge Street, turn right on to Castle Street, turn on to Old Edinburgh Road, turn left on to Mitchell's Lane, turn left on to Argyle Street, turn left on to Gordon Terrace.

STB rating Hotel *

RIVERSIDE HOUSE HOTEL

8 Ness Bank, Inverness IV2 4SF

Tel (01463) 231052

E-mail hotel@ardmuir.demon.co.uk

Website www.ibmpcug.co.uk/-ecs/guest/

Open All year

Rooms 5 single, 3 double, 3 twin, 5 en-suite.

Prices B&B – single, £30; double/twin, £30; B&B plus evening meal, £40.

Ver TV in room; tea/coffee facilities; evening meal available; pay phone available; liquor licence; use of lounge; hairdryer and iron.

Non-ver Packed lunches by arrangement; vegetarian meals available; pets welcome by arrangement; use of shower, iron and clothes-drying facilities.

Location Ness Bank (C4).

Directions From Ness Bridge (C3) turn left on to Castle Road, take the first right turning on to Ness Bank.

STB rating Hotel **

STATION HOTEL

18 Academy Street, Inverness IV1 1LG

Tel (01463) 231926   *Fax* (01463) 710705

E-mail shi@dial.pipex.com

Open All year

Rooms 31 single, 6 double, 23 twin, 7 family, 42 en-suite, 14 private facility.

Prices B&B – single, £65; double/twin, £99 (room price); B&B plus evening meal, £127.

Ver TV in room; tea/coffee facilities; non-smoking; telephone in room; limited parking; evening meal available; room service; laundry service; use of hairdryer.

Non-ver Packed lunches by arrangement; vegetarian and special diets available; pets welcome by arrangement; use of shower, baby's cot, iron and clothes-drying facilities.

Location Academy Street (C2).

Directions From Ness Bridge (C3) at Ness Bridge turn right on to Bank Street, turn right on to Friar's Lane, take the second right turning on to Academy Street.

STB rating Hotel **

TOWER HOTEL

4 Ardross Street, Inverness IV3 5NQ

Tel (01463) 232765   *Fax* (01463) 232970

Open All year

Rooms 2 single, 4 double, 3 twin, 3 family, all en-suite.

Prices B&B – single, £30–£48; double/twin, £25–£35; B&B plus evening meal, £38–£48.

Ver TV in room; tea/coffee facilities; telephone in room; limited parking; evening meal available; laundry service.

Non-ver Packed lunches by arrangement; vegetarian and special diets by arrangement; use of baby's cot and iron; credit/debit cards accepted.

Location Ardross Street (B3).

Directions From Ness Bridge (C3) cross Ness Bridge, follow Young Street on to Tomnahurich Street, take first left turning after

Ardross Place.

Comments Superbly situated on the River Ness, opposite the castle and a few minutes' walk from Eden Court Theatre and the town centre. Warm welcome and a friendly, attentive service. All rooms en-suite. The Riverside Restaurant offers an excellent selection of Scottish and European cuisine.

STB rating Hotel **

WINDSOR TOWN HOUSE HOTEL

22 Ness Bank, Inverness IV2 4SF

Tel (01463) 715535   *Fax* (01463) 713262

Open All year (restricted Christmas and New Year opening).

Rooms 3 single, 3 double, 2 twin, 2 family, 10 private facility.

Prices B&B – single, £35–£75; double/twin, £25–£60; B&B plus evening meal, £50–£90.

Ver TV in room with satellite facility; tea/coffee facilities; telephone in room; non-smoking; private parking; use of hairdryer.

Non-ver Vegetarian meals available; use of baby's cot and iron; credit/debit cards accepted.

Location Ness Bank (C4).

Directions From Ness Bridge (C3) at Ness Bridge turn left on to Castle Road, take the first right turning on to Ness Bank.

Comments This traditional, comfortable town house hotel is ideally situated on the lovely River Ness opposite the Cathedral. Short riverside walk to town centre. Attractive en-suite bedrooms. Riverside breakfast observatory. Free private car park. Spring and autumn breaks.

STB rating Hotel ***

CAMPING AND CARAVAN PARKS

Prices are given where available, but as the Scottish Tourist Board have not verified that caravan and camping sites provide the facilities they claim to provide, it would be in your interest to telephone and enquire beforehand.

AUCHNAHALLIN CARAVAN AND CAMPING CENTRE

Daviot East, Inverness-shire IV1 2XQ

Tel (01463) 772286   *Fax* (01463) 72282

E-mail auch@zetnet.co.uk

Website www.users.zetnet.co.uk/auch/
Open Easter to October
Pitches 65 caravans (18 caravans, sleeping 4–6, £135–£310 per week). 20 tent pitches (£4.50–£9 per pitch, per night).
STB rating ✔✔✔

BUGHT CARAVAN AND CAMPING SITE
The Bught, Inverness IV3 5SR
Tel (01463) 236920   *Fax* (01463) 712850
Open April to September
Pitches 90 touring pitches. £3.10–£9.30 per pitch, per night.
STB rating ✔✔✔

BUNCHREW CARAVAN PARK
Bunchrew, Inverness IV3 6TD
Tel (01463) 237802   *Fax* (01463) 225803
Open 20 March to 13 December
Pitches 125 touring pitches. £4–£8.50 per pitch per night. 14 caravans,sleeping 6, £114–£240 per week.
STB rating ✔✔✔

CULLODEN MOOR CARAVAN CLUB SITE
Newlands, Culloden Moor, IV1 2EF
Tel (01463) 790625
Open April to October
Pitches 100 touring pitches. £5–£12.80 per pitch, per night.
Location Culloden, near Westhill.
STB rating ✔✔✔✔

LOVAT BRIDGE CARAVAN PARK
Lovat Bridge, Beauly, Inverness-shire
Tel (01463) 782374
Open March to October
Pitches 40 touring pitches. £6–£8 per pitch, per night.
STB rating ✔✔✔

SCANIPORT CARAVAN AND CAMPING PARK
Scaniport, By Inverness IV1 2DL
Tel (01463) 751351
Open Easter to September

Pitches 30 touring pitches. £4–£7 per pitch, per night.
STB rating ✔✔✔

TORVEAN CARAVAN PARK
Glenurquhart Road, Inverness IV3 6HY
Tel (01463) 220582   *Fax* (01463) 821382
Open April to October
Pitches 50 touring pitches. £8.50–£9.50 per pitch, per night. 10
    holiday caravans sleeping 2–5, £160–£295 per week.
Comments A small, secluded park on the banks of the Caledonian
    Canal, overlooking Torvean golf course. An ideal base for
    exploring Loch Ness and the West Coast. Within walking
    distance of shops, theatre, swimming pool, sports centre, Floral
    Hall and the Ness Islands. Cruises available on Loch Ness. On
    the bus route, Torvean is adjacent to the Loch Ness Hotel on
    the A82, one and a half miles from the town centre, on the
    right-hand side.
STB rating ✔✔✔✔

STUDENT AND YOUTH HOSTELS
BAZPACKERS HOSTEL
4 Culduthel Road, Inverness IV2 4AB
Tel (01463) 717663
Open All year
Rooms 7 rooms, 30 beds.
Prices £7.50–£9 per night.
Location Culduthel Road (C4).
Directions From Ness Bridge (C3) follow Bridge Street, turn right
    on to Castle Street, continue on to Culduthel Road.

DALNEIGH HALL
St Ninian Drive, Inverness IV3 5AU
Tel (01463) 239753
Open All year
Rooms 66 rooms, 84 beds.
Prices £7–£12.50 per person, per night.
Directions From Ness Bridge (C3) to St Ninian Drive follow
    Young Street on to Tomnahurich Street, away from the town
    centre, take the third right turning on to Bruce Gardens and
    continue to the end, turn right on to St Valery Street, turn right

on to St Ninian Drive.

EASTGATE HOSTEL
38 Eastgate, Inverness IV2 3NA
Tel (01463) 718756   *Fax* (01463) 718756
Open All year
Rooms 8 rooms, 38 beds.
Price £8.90 per person, per night.
Location C3

INVERNESS STUDENT HOSTEL
8 Culduthel Road, Inverness IV2 4AB
Tel (01463) 236556
Open All year
Rooms 9 rooms, 57 beds.
Price £9.50–£10.50 per person, per night.
Location C4
Directions From Ness Bridge (C3) follow Bridge Street, turn right
on to Castle Street, continue on to Culduthel Road.

INVERNESS YOUTH HOSTEL
Victoria Drive, Inverness IV2 3QB
Tel (01463) 231771   *Fax* (01463) 710349
Open All year
Rooms 35 rooms, 166 beds.
Prices Telephone for details.
Location Victoria Drive (D2/E2).
Directions From Ness Bridge (C3) turn right at Ness Bridge on to
Bank Street, turn right on to Friar's Lane, take second right
turning on to Academy Street, take first left on to Millburn
Road, continue for a time, then take first right past the Eastgate
Centre on to Victoria Drive.

SELF-CATERING ACCOMMODATION
These properties are to rent. No map reference is given as the
property address differs from that of the owner.

S. ABRAHAM
Warrendale, Daviot Muir, Daviot, Inverness-shire IV1 3ER
Tel (01463) 772016   *Fax* (01463) 772084

Open All year
Property 1 house, 4 bedrooms, property sleeps 7.
Price £80–£425 per week.
STB rating Self-catering **

MRS J. ALEXANDER
Blackpark Farm, Westhill, Inverness IV1 2BP
Tel (01463) 790620   *Fax* (01463) 794262
Open April to October
Property 1 caravan, 2 bedrooms, property sleeps 2–6.
Price £150 per week.
STB rating Award pending.

MRS M. BALLANTYNE
96 Diriebught Road, Inverness IV2 3QN
Tel (01463) 224363
Open May to October
Property 1 cottage, 1 bedroom, property sleeps 2–4.
Price £160–£190 per week.
STB rating Self-catering **

CLAVA LODGE HOLIDAY HOMES
Culloden Moor, Inverness IV1 2EJ
Tel (01463) 790228   *Fax* (01463) 790228
E-mail enquiries@clavalodge.demon.co.uk
Website www.clavalodge.demon.co.uk
Open All year
Property 5 cottages, 2 chalets, 4 flats, 1 log cabin, 1–3 bedrooms,
     property sleeps 2–5.
Price £130–£395 per week.
STB rating Self-catering **

CONNEL COURT
3 Connel Court, Ardconnel Street, Inverness IV2 3EY
Tel (01463) 237086 or (0421) 937942
Open All year
Property 1 flat, 2 bedrooms, property sleeps 4–5.
Price £200–£360 per week.
STB rating Self-catering ****

Rowan Glen, Culbokie, Dingwall, Ross-shire IV7 8JY
Tel (01349) 877762
E-mail 106770.3175@compuserve.com
Open All year
Property 2 flats, 2 bedrooms, property sleeps 4.
Price £210–£390 per week.
STB rating Self-catering – 1st flat ***; 2nd flat ****

MR M.R. FRASER
Reelig Estate, Kirkhill, Inverness-shire IV5 7PR
Tel (01463) 831208   *Fax* (01463) 831413
E-mail reelig@aol.com
Open March to November
Property 2 cottages, 11 chalets, 1 bungalow, 1 flat, properties sleep
    from 4–5.
Price £135–£350 per week.
Comments Character cottages and cedar chalets set individually in
    lovely old Highland estate. Ideal for touring the Highlands.
    Storage heating included – for other electricity there is a £1
    coin meter.
STB rating Self-catering * to **

FUARANBUIE
8 Kinerras, Kiltarlity, by Beauly, Inverness-shire IV4 7JL
Tel (01463) 741261
Open April to October
Property 1 flat, 2 bedrooms, property sleeps 2–4.
Price £200 per week.
Comments Fuaranbuie is situated next to the owner's cottage on a
    quiet country road with magnificent views of Strathglass.
    Ideally situated for walking, golf and fishing.
STB rating Self-catering ***

MRS C.M. GRANT
44 Island Bank Road, Inverness IV2 4QT
Tel (01463) 230792
Open May to October
Property 1 flat, 1 bedroom, property sleeps 1–2.
Price £125–£135 per week.

STB rating Self-catering **

58 Drummond Road, Inverness IV2 4NU
Tel (01463) 232468
Open April to September
Property 1 caravan, property sleeps 8.
Prices £130–£230 per week.
STB rating Award pending.

Clach Bhan, Loaneckhein, Kiltarlity, Beauly, Inverness-shire
   IV4 7JQ
Tel (01463) 741328
Open April to October
Property 1 cottage, 2 bedrooms, property sleeps 4.
Prices £110–£230 per week.
STB rating Self-catering **

Blackpark Farm, Lechkin, Inverness IV3 8PW
Tel (01463) 241831   *Fax* (01463) 241885
Open April to October
Property 3 caravans, 2 bedrooms, property sleeps 2–6.
Price £140–£230 per week.
STB rating Award pending.

Westview House, Upper Myrtleside, Nairnside, Inverness
   IV1 2BP
Tel (01463) 794228   *Fax* (01463) 794228
Open All year
Property 1 apartment, 1 family bedroom, property sleeps 4.
Price £200–£250 per week.
STB rating Self-catering ****

Kingillie House, Kirkhill, Inverness IV5 7PU
Tel (01463) 831275   *Fax* (01463) 831550
Open April to September

Property 2 cottages, 2–4 bedrooms, property sleeps 4–6.
Price £170–£325 per week.
STB rating Self-catering **

LENTRAN HOLIDAY COTTAGES
c/o MacKay's Agency, 30 Frederick Street, Edinburgh, EH2 2JR
Tel (0131) 225 2539   *Fax* (0131) 226 5284
Open May to October
Property 3 cottages, 2–3 bedrooms, property sleeps 4–16.
Price £145–£350 per week.
STB rating Self-catering **

MRS A. MACKENZIE
6a Green Drive, Inverness IV2 4EX
Tel (01463) 236763
Open All year
Property 1 bungalow, 3 bedrooms, property sleeps 5.
Price £110–£300 per week.
STB rating Self-catering **

MERLEWOOD HOUSE
Merlewood Road, Inverness IV2 4NL
Tel (01463) 236060
Open All year
Property 1 cottage, 1 bedroom, property sleeps 2.
Price £115–£290 per week.
STB rating Award pending.

MRS E.E. MURRAY
18 Wellside Road, Balloch, Inverness IV1 2GS
Tel (01463) 793492
Open All year
Property 1 flat, 2 bedrooms, property sleeps 1–4.
Price £240–£350 per week.
STB rating Award pending.

THE NEUK
Kilmuir, 17 Ness Bank, Inverness IV2 4SF
Tel (01463) 712266
Open April to October

Property 1 cottage, 3 bedrooms, property sleeps 6.

Price £270–£370 per week.

Comments A traditional 1830 seafront cottage, 6 miles from Inverness in a peaceful location but not isolated. The ideal base from which to tour the Scottish Highlands. Magnificent views to the south across the Moray Firth.

STB rating Self-catering **

PINE CHALETS (Mr Campbell)

Lentran, by Inverness IV3 6RN

Tel (01764) 652951   *Fax* (01764) 654537

Open All year

Property 5 chalets, 2 bedrooms, property sleeps 4 – 5.

Price £150–£320 per week.

Comments Peaceful location, five lovely two-bedroom chalets set on a tranquil hillside with panoramic views overlooking the sea and the Highland mountains. Located on a quiet country lane, secluded and safe for children and pets. Ideal for all activities, touring or relaxing. Inverness – seven miles; Beauly – five miles. Fully equipped including colour TV, microwave and washing machine. Brochure available.

STB rating Self-catering **

MR AND MRS R.M. POTTIE

Easter Dalziel Farm, Dalcross, Inverness IV1 2JL

Tel (01667) 462213   *Fax* (01667) 462213

Open All year

Property 3 cottages, 3 bedrooms, property sleeps 4–6.

Price £120–£410 per week.

Comments Fully equipped cottages on 200-acre stock/arable farm, seven miles east of Inverness. Superb central location from which to explore the Highlands, long or short break. Brochure available.

STB rating Self-catering *** to ****

RIVANA HOUSE

Copperfield, Culloden Road, Westhill, Inverness IV1 2BQ

Tel (01463) 792780 or (0411) 237676

Fax (01463) 792780

E-mail nickp@cali.co.uk

Open All year

Property 1 house, 1 cottage, 2–5 bedrooms, property sleeps 4–9.

Price £175–£450 per week.

Comments Charming property ideally situated on the banks of the River Ness in the heart of the Highland capital. Only a few minutes' walk to shops, bus and rail stations. Secluded garden equipped with barbecue and garden furniture is a real sun trap offering total relaxation. Private parking. The house is perfect for large families (five bedrooms) and the cottage for couples and small families (two bedrooms).

STB rating Self-catering ***

TORGUISH HOLIDAY HOMES

Torguish House, Daviot, Inverness IV1 2XQ

Tel (01463) 772208   *Fax* (01463) 7722308

E-mail self.catering@torguish.com

Website www.torguish.com/

Open All year

Property 4 cottages, 1–2 bedrooms, property sleeps 2–4.

Price £120–£295 per week.

Comments Torguish Holiday Homes, set in the grounds of Torguish House, the once family home of late author Alistair McLean, who wrote many famous novels. The steading has been converted into four compact cottages, all fully equipped, situated approximately five miles south of Inverness. Ideal location for touring, walking, fishing, golfing, skiing, or just to relax in the garden.

STB rating Self-catering ***

WHERE TO EAT

RESTAURANTS

CASTLE RESTAURANT
Tel (01463) 230925
Fax (01463) 230925
41 Castle Street (C3)
Personal Recommendation:
Friendly family-run restaurant,
quick and efficient with a
welcoming atmosphere.
Freshly prepared food.
Breakfast, lunch, dinner,
coffee, tea, home baking.

LE DÉJÀ VU
Tel (01463) 231075
Fax (01463) 231075
38 Eastgate (C3)
French restaurant serving
traditional French provincial
food, specialising in meat, fish
and seafood, pierrade and
fondues. Full à la carte menu
available.

DICKENS RESTAURANT INTERNATIONAL
Tel (01463) 713111
Fax (01463) 713111
77-79 Church Street (C2)
International cuisine. Specialist
dishes. French, Chinese,
vegetarian, local dishes. Air
conditioning. All welcome,
including small parties.

FINLAY'S
Tel (01463) 245981
Fax (01463) 245982
18 Tomnahurich Street (B3)
Public house serving lunches
and evening meals. Also
includes entertainment and
children's licence.

GLEN MOHR HOTEL RESTAURANTS
Tel (01463) 234308
Fax (01463) 713170
9-12 Ness Bank (D4/D3)
Riverview Restaurant and
Nico's Bistro for Scottish food,
including fresh seafood and
ethnic cuisine. Credit/debit
cards accepted. Non-smoking.
Restricted liquor licence.
Vegetarian meals available.
May be booked through a
travel agent.

GUNSMITHS (PUB AND RESTAURANT)
Tel (01463) 710519
Fax (01463) 794486
30 Union Street (C2)

HARRY RAMSDEN'S
Tel (01463) 713345
Fax (01463) 713417
Beechwood Business Park
Directions See Damfield Road
(D4/E4), follow on to
Culcabock Road, follow on to
Old Perth Road, continue
straight through the ring road,
following signs for Culloden,
and Beechwood Business Park
is on the left.
200-seater restaurant and
takeaway. Fully licensed.

HEATHMOUNT HOTEL AND RESTAURANTS
Tel (01463) 235877
Fax (01463) 715749
Kingsmills Road (D3)
Newly refurbished restaurants
(smoking and non-smoking),
offer à la carte menu.

LITTLEJOHN'S
Tel (01463) 713005
Fax (01463) 712930
28-30 Church Street (C2)
Themed family restaurant,
catering for all tastes and age
groups. Working model trains
for the kids to see.

LORIMER'S FAMILY RESTAURANT
Tel (01463) 717717
Longman Road (C1)
Includes takeaway, from fish
and chips to pastas, from bur-
gers to chicken, from

gammon steaks to traditional
meals.

MOLLOYS
Tel (01463) 233307
50 Baron Taylor's Street (C3)
Public house and popular
eating place open for meals
9 a.m. to 9 p.m., upstairs and
downstairs. Families welcome.
Function room also available.

THE PANCAKE PLACE
Tel (01463) 226156
25-27 Church Street (C2)
Coffee shop and restaurant.
Breakfast, brunch, lunches,
super sweets, coffee.

PEKING HOUSE TAKEAWAY RESTAURANT
Tel (01463) 224467
31 Castle Street (C3)

QISMAT TANDOORI RESTAURANT
Tel (01463) 716020
1b Millburn Road (D2)
Freshly prepared Indian meals.
Phone orders welcome. Local
delivery.

THE RIVERHOUSE RESTAURANT
Tel (01463) 222033
1 Greig Street (B3), off
Kenneth Street.
Quality restaurant with fish
specialities.

CAFÉS

CHARLIE'S CAFÉ
Tel: (01463) 233498
Within bus station, Margaret
Street (C2)

CHIMES TEAROOM
Tel: (01463) 719181
8a Stephen's Brae, near
Eastgate (B2/B3)

MANNA HOUSE TEAROOM
Tel: (01463) 710710
48 Huntly Street (B2/B3)

THE MARKET CAFÉ
Tel: (01463) 717623

10-12 Market Arcade,
Academy Street (C2)
Small but friendly tearooms
within the Market Arcade,
serving tea, coffee and meals.

OLIVER'S COFFEE SHOP AND BAKERY
Tel: (01463) 232664
High Street (C3)
Clean, friendly café with both
smoking and non-smoking
sections.

TAKEAWAYS

ACADEMY TAKEAWAY
Tel: (01463) 231078
107 Academy Street (C2)

ANNE'S TAKEAWAY
Tel: (01463) 232975
Market Close (C2)

BITI'S
Tel: (01463) 233445
13 Young Street (B3/C3)
The Highlands' number one
pizza place. Takeaway and
delivery.

BURGER KING
Tel: (01463) 712223
2-6 Inglis Street (C3)

CASA ITALIA
Tel: (01463) 712678
2 Young Street (B3/C3)
Traditional Italian pizza.
Home delivery and takeaway.

CHARLIE'S
Tel: (01463) 232498
29 Grant Street (B1)

CHARLIE CHAN'S
Tel: (01463) 232884/717778

CHINA COTTAGE
Tel: (01463) 710740
40 Eastgate (B1)

CRUMBS
Tel: (01463) 715062
19 Inglis Street (C2)

DENIS'S
Tel (01463) 232279
7 Wells Street (B2)
Finest Cantonese and Peking
cuisine. Delicious Chinese hot
meals. Takeaway or delivery.

EVERGREEN CHINESE
TAKEAWAY
Tel (01463) 711376
26 Grant Street (B1)

HONG KONG KITCHEN
Tel (01463) 712565
105 Academy Street (C2)

INVERNESS INDIAN
TANDOORI
Tel (01463) 220567
38 Waterloo Place (B1)

KEBAB HOUSE
Tel (01463) 713842
42 Eastgate (C3)

KHAN'S 3 IN 1
Tel (01463) 238400
19 Grant Street (B1)

MCDONALD'S
Tel (01463) 237499
High Street (C3)

MR CHIPS
Tel (01463) 233544
37a Telford Road (A2)

MR RICE
Tel (01463) 715575
37b Telford Street

1ST PIZZA DIRECT
Tel (01463) 717171
Glenurquhart Road (A5)

SNAX
Tel (01463) 718037
36 Grant Street (B1)

WELCOME
Tel (01463) 232017
10 Greig Street (B3)
Chinese hot food takeaway.
Home delivery service.

WEST END CHIPPIES
Tel (01463) 232903
19 Young Street (B3/C3)

ENTERTAINMENT

PUBLIC HOUSES

FINLAYS
Tel (01463) 245981
Fax (01463) 245982
18 Tomnahurich Street (B3)

GUNSMITHS
Tel (01463) 710519
30 Union Street (C2)

JOHNNY FOXES IRISH PUB
Tel (01463) 236577
26 Bank Street (C2/C3)
Live music, a restaurant area
and a very welcoming
atmosphere.

MOLLOYS
Tel (01463) 233307
50 Baron Taylor's Square (C2/
C3)

NUMBER 27
Tel (01463) 241999
27 Castle Street (C3)
Public house also open for tea,
coffee and full meals available
in restaurant area.

THEATRES AND CINEMAS

EDEN COURT
THEATRE/CINEMA
Tel (01463) 234234
Fax (01463) 713810
Bishop's Road (B4)
Includes exhibitions, café, bar.
A wide-ranging programme
throughout the year.

LA SCALA (CALEDONIAN
CINEMAS)
Tel (01463) 233302
Strothers Lane (C2)

WARNER VILLAGE CINEMAS
Tel (01463) 711147 (recorded
information and card
bookings)
Inverness Retail and Business
Park. From Millburn Road
(D2) follow on to ring road
and continue straight through
on to A96 following signs for
Nairn.
Seven-screen multiplex, five
minutes' drive from town
centre.

NIGHTCLUBS

G'S NIGHTCLUB & THE NILE BAR

9-21 Castle Street, Inverness
IV2 3DX
Tel (01463) 233322
Fax (01463) 711556
Usual age group 18–30
Dress code Smart but casual. No trainers on Saturday nights.
Monday night 9.30 p.m. to 1.30 a.m. Entry fee £2 with discount for students. Lots of great bar bargains.
Tuesday/Wednesday night Closed.
Thursday night 9.30 p.m. to 1.30 a.m. Entry fee £2. Selected drinks from £1.20. Thursday is '70s night.
Friday night 9.30 p.m. to 1.30 a.m. Entry fee £3. A night of commercial dance tunes.
Saturday night 9.30 p.m. to 1.30 a.m. Entry fee £5. A night of commercial dance tunes.
Sunday night 9 p.m. to midnight. Entry free. Hard dance tunes.
Websites: www.nessweb.co.uk and www.charleston43. freeserve.co.uk

WHERE TO GO AND WHAT TO SEE IN AND AROUND INVERNESS

Inverness and the surrounding district offers much to the visitor to see and do. From historical sites to garden centres and floral displays, public parks and all manner of arts and crafts – including many where you can visit the workshops and watch the wares being handcrafted.

There are many excellent attractions outside Inverness and Loch Ness and, while some are mentioned here, this is by no means an exhaustive list. The Tourist Information Centre at Castle Wynd, Inverness, will be able to help with information on these attractions as well as on accommodation in these areas.

Fort William town is a popular holiday destination all year round. Brushed by the Gulf Stream, the town enjoys a mild climate all year, while the winter snow provides superb skiing conditions. There are many visitor attractions, including the Highland Mystery World tour complete with café and gift shop, Seal Island cruises, Glen Nevis Visitor Centre, Treasures of the Earth (a simulation of caves, caverns, mining scenes and priceless collections of gemstones and crystals) and the Nevis Range of Mountains (which include four of the five highest mountains in Britain) in all their glory. For more information contact Fort William and Lochaber Tourist Office, *Tel* (01397) 703781.

The sites below are listed alphabetically.

IDEAS FOR DAYS OUT

BALNAIN HOUSE
40 Huntly Street, Inverness IV3 5HR
Tel (01463) 715757 *Fax* (01463) 713611
Open Summer, 10 a.m. to 5 p.m. (7 days, with music most evenings); session nights are Tuesdays and Wednesdays. Winter, 10 a.m. to 5 p.m. Tuesdays to Saturdays; session night, Thursday.

Home of Highland music. Learn to play the bagpipes and other Highland instruments and learn about the history of Highland music. Audio-visual exhibition, Celtic music shop, performances, workshops, classes in playing and dancing, café/bar (fresh seafood, vegetarian specialities, prime Scottish beef and lamb; fresh Scottish fayre). For reservations telephone Café Balnain on (01463) 225585.

CASTLE GARRISON ENCOUNTER

Inverness Castle (rear entrance). Approach from Castle Wynd, off Castle Street, Inverness

For further information 3 Connel Court, Ardconnel Street, Inverness IV2 3EY

Tel (01463) 24363 *Fax* (01463) 710755

Open March to November

Personal Recommendation Why not try the guided tour of Inverness Castle, accompanied by historical characters (who really do look the part!), including a military storekeeper welcoming you as a 'new recruit', a soldier's wife explaining the role of women in this period, and a no-nonsense sergeant who teaches sword fighting as he trains men to become soldiers for the last Jacobite rising? Both educational and entertaining. Highly recommended.

CAWDOR CASTLE

Cawdor, Nairn, IV12 5RD

Tel (01667) 404615   *Fax* (01667) 404674

Open 1 May to the second Sunday in October, 10a.m. to 5p.m.

A fairytale castle which has remained the home of the Thanes of Cawdor ever since it was built in 1370. There are beautiful gardens, nature trails, a nine-hole golf course, restaurant, gift shop, wool shop, book shop, snack bar and a picnic area, ensuring a fun day out for the whole family. Credit/debit cards accepted, private parking, non-smoking, vegetarian meals available, restricted liquor licence. Highly commended by the Scottish Tourist Board.

CLAVA CAIRNS

Inverness (follow the signs for Culloden)

A notable group of burial cairns of late-Neolithic or Bronze Age near Culloden Moor. The whole area is rich in similar types of field monuments, and further details can be gained from the Tourist Information Centre, Castle Wynd, Inverness.

CRAIG PHADRIG FORT AND FOREST

See Kenneth Street (A2), follow Kenneth Street to ring road, continue on to Telford Street. Cross the Muirtown Bridge, take second left turning on to King Brude Road, take third right turning on to Leachkin (say 'Larkin') Road. Follow sign for Craig Dunain, continue up the hill and take the first right turning into the Craig Phadrig car park.

CROMWELL'S TOWER AND REMAINS OF CROMWELL'S FORT

Cromwell Road, Inverness

See Shore Street (B1), continue on to Cromwell Road, Cromwell's site of clock Tower is on the right-hand side. Although the site is not generally open to the public, there are some interesting wall markings left by Cromwell's soldiers.

CULLODEN MOOR VISITOR CENTRE

Culloden Moor, Inverness IV2 5EU

Tel (01463) 790607

The Battle of Culloden Moor was the last pitched battle fought on British soil, as Prince Charles Edward Stuart's supporters were defeated by the Duke of Cumberland's forces. The National Trust for Scotland has restored the battlefield to how it was on the day of the battle. The Visitor Centre has a display of weapons and other objects dating from the time of the battle. Also on show is a colourful historical display, an audio-visual programme in six languages, and an on-site shop and restaurant.

Access for wheelchair users and people with disabilities.

FORT GEORGE

Ardersier, Inverness IV1 2TD

Tel (01667) 462777   *Fax* (01667) 462698

Built following the Battle of Culloden, Fort George stands on the coast and is still in use today. The outstanding military fortifications, enclosing an area of 42 acres, is a must-see for any visitor to the Highlands. Commended by the Scottish Tourist Board.

Follow the A96 trunk road out of Inverness, turn left on to the B9039 following signs for Dalcross and Inverness Airport, then continue on to Ardersier and Fort George.

(at the south end of Loch Oich), Great Glen Water Park, South Laggen, near Spean Bridge, PH34 4EA

Tel (01809) 501381 or contact Monster Activities, *Tel* (01320) 366508

E-mail Ian@macmonster.freeserve.co.uk

Website www.monsteractivities.com

Ideal for families and young children (the Little Monster Kids Club). Participate in a range of activities, including abseiling, archery, air rifle shooting, canoeing and kayaking, clay pigeon shooting, juggling and circus skills, motor boating, pedalo (pedal-boats), white-water rafting, mountain bike touring, snow-boarding, guided walks and navigation, sailing, orienteering, windsurfing, water-skiing, jet-biking, tennis and kite-building. With equipment for hire – fishing rods (not including tackle), mountain bikes (including helmet), wetsuits and swimming buoyancy aids for one, two or three hours or all day.

Kincraig, Inverness-shire PH21 1NL

Tel (01540) 651270 for further information.

Many animals on display at a drive-through reserve, including those which were once native to the Highlands. A 'safari' experience, with large herds of roe deer and red deer, Highland cattle, wild horses and bison roaming freely throughout the reserve. Walk-around habitats in special enclosures, featuring reindeer, Arctic foxes, otters, wildcat, lynx, badgers and owls and 'Wolf Territory', a raised walkway leading you into the heart of the wolf enclosure.

The visitor centre includes an exhibition, cafeteria overlooking the wildfowl lochan and a gift shop full of wildlife souvenirs.

Unit 2, 42 Harbour Road, Inverness,

Tel (01463) 713134

Open 7 days a week, 11 a.m. to 6 p.m.

A children's soft play area (1–12 years of age). Separate area for toddlers.

INVERNESS MUSEUM AND ART GALLERY
Castle Wynd, Inverness IV2 3EB

Tel (01463) 237114   *Fax* (01463) 225293

Open All year, Monday to Saturday, 9 a.m. to 5 p.m.

Museum depicts the history of the Highlands and the art collection also offers interesting old views of Inverness. Admission free.

NESS ISLANDS

Tranquil islands with a bridge crossing from either side of the banks of the River Ness – and between each of these islands – offering peaceful walks for all. See Ness Islands (B6/B5).

Cyclists, walkers and horse-riders are welcome at Inverness area Forests. Telephone (01320) 366322 for free leaflets on many different areas The Great Glen Cycle Route (from Inverness to Fort Augustus); the Great Glen Forest Walk, Skye and Lochalsh, Portree/Alphabet Trail, Glen Affric Forest Walks, Kylerhea Otter Haven, the Isle of Raasay. Horse riding permits by arrangements.

PUBLIC PARKS, GARDENS AND FLORAL DISPLAYS

Public glasshouses and gardens, tropical glasshouses, cactus house and demonstration gardens. Visitor centre and café. Opening hours vary. Commended by the Scottish Tourist Board.

BELLFIELD PARK

Includes putting green and tennis courts (C4/C5)

BIRCH HOUSE HERBS

Tigh Bea, Kiltarlity, Inverness-shire IV4 7JH

Tel (01463) 741425

Open April to October, 9 a.m. to 6 p.m.

A new nursery and garden selling a variety of herbs and wild flowers for culinary, medicinal and other uses.

Location Kiltarlity (B1)

BUGHT FLORAL HALL

Bught Lane, Bught Park, Inverness IV3 5SS

Tel (01463) 222755

Fax (01463) 712593

Open All year

HOWDEN'S GARDEN CENTRE

Telford Street, Inverness IV3 5LF
Tel (01463) 711134
Fax (01463) 226423
Open All year

Superb collection of plants and everything else to make the most of your garden. Coffee shop with home baking – hot food all day.

ARTS, CRAFTS AND GIFTS

CELTIC CRAFT CENTRE

15 Inglis Street, IV1 1HN
Tel (01463) 713123
Fax (01463) 234406
A wonderful range of Celtic gifts and jewellery available at shops in Inverness and Skye.

CREATIONS

13 Market Hall, Inverness IV1 1PJ
Tel (01463) 241902
Open All year, Monday to Saturday, 9.30 a.m. to 5.30 p.m.
A wide range of needlework kits, including many Scottish and local. Other crafts also available.

CROFT 7

The Workshop
Inchmore, Kirkhill, Inverness IV5 7PX
Tel (01463) 831320
Fax (01463) 831320
Open All year, Tuesday, Thursday and Saturday, 10 a.m. to 5 p.m.
Wool and wood craft workshops, spinning

demonstrations, native woodland exhibition, handcrafted textiles.

D. & H. NORVAL GIFTS AND CRAFTS

Dunbars Hospital, 88 Church Street, Inverness IV1 1EF
Tel (01463) 232739
Open All year, six days a week, 9 a.m. to 5.30 p.m.
From Ness Bridge (C3) turn right on to Bank Street and turn right on to Friar's Lane. Dunbars Hospital is on the right at the junction of the two right turns to Church Street and Academy Street.

HIGHLAND AROMATICS

Inchmore, Kirkhill, Inverness IV5 7PX
Tel (01463) 831625
Fax (01463) 831405
Open All year, except for Christmas and New Year, Monday to Thursday, 10 a.m. to 4 p.m.; Friday, 10 a.m. to 3 p.m.
Visitors may see the making of fine perfumed soaps. Phone

if party numbers are over ten.

HIGHLAND WINERIES
Moniack Castle, Kirkhill,
Inverness IV5 7PQ
Tel (01463) 831283
Fax (01463) 831419
Open All year Monday to
Saturday, 10 a.m. to 5 p.m.
Castle producing wines,
liqueurs and preserves,
includes visitor centre. Open
for tours and tastings.

HOBBY HAVEN
8 Drummond Street,
Inverness IV1 1BD
Tel (01463) 714724
Fax (01463) 714724
Supplier of craft materials
stitchcraft, art-stamping,
parchment craft, quilting,
decoupage, beads, paints.

JAMES PRINGLE WEAVERS OF
INVERNESS
Holm Mills, Dores Road,
Inverness IV2 4RB
Tel (01463) 223311
Fax (01463) 231042
Open All year
Weaving mill producing
tartan rugs. Extensive mill
shop with quality brand
names. Clan Tartan centre and
a large restaurant.
Commended by the Scottish
Tourist Board. See Haugh
Road (C4), continue on to
Island Bank Road, and follow
on to Dores Road, and Holm
Woollen Mills is on your
right.

JOE LINDSAY –
TARGEMAKER
Balquhidder, Main Street,
North Kessock, Inverness IV1
1XN
Tel (01463) 731577
Targes are high quality,
handcrafted, full-size
reproductions of original
Highlanders' shields.
Embossed leather fronts with
brass nails, bosses, paltes and
spikes, deerskin backs with
handle and armstrap. Boxed
with history ticket. Targes are
collectors' items, priced from
£30 to £230. Worldwide mail
order service available. Visitors
always welcome to
Balquhidder – please phone
first. For North Kessock, see
Inverness (C1), join the A9
trunk road from Daviot and
cross Kessock Bridge, which
spans Beauly Firth and Moray
Firth, then continue on to
North Kessock.

NORTHERN LIGHTS
CANDLES
Lentran, by Inverness
IV3 6RL
Tel (01463) 831332
Open April to October;
summer 10 a.m. to 7 p.m.;
winter 12 noon to 6 p.m.

A range of decorative
candles all handmade in the
workshop. Visitors
welcome.

PETER TYLER
(WOODTURNER)
Milton of Tordarroch,
Dunlichity, Farr, by Inverness

IV1 2XF
Tel (01808) 521414
Open April to December,
Monday to Saturday, 10 a.m.
to 5.30 p.m.
Large range of woodturned
items produced in workshop.
Adjacent shop also has other
local crafts.

ART GALLERIES

KILMORACK GALLERY
By Beauly, Inverness-shire
IV4 7AL
Tel (01463) 783230
Open April to January
The Highlands' largest
exhibition space, showing the
work of the Highlands' top
contemporary artists.

THE RIVERSIDE GALLERY
11 Bank Street, Inverness
IV1 1QY
Tel (01463) 224781
Open All year, Monday to
Saturday, 9 a.m. to 5.30 p.m.
Gallery specialising in the sale
of paintings, prints and
sculptures by local artists.

TOURS AND SIGHTSEEING

DROVERS GUIDED WALKS
70 Mason Road, Inverness
Tel (01463) 242095
Open March to October
Guided walks in the
spectacular scenery of the
Scottish Highlands.

GORDON'S MINIBUS
Heather Cottage, North
Kessock, Inverness
Tel (01463) 731202
Open All year
Fresh-air tour to Loch Ness.
Easy walking (optional).
Urquhart Castle, heather
moors, history, nature. No
tourist shops.

FORBES MINICOACH SERVICE
30 Darris Road, Inverness
Tel (01463) 236719
Open January to December
Day tours and private hire
specialists in small group
travel.

GUIDE FRIDAY TOURS

Inverness Railway Station (office), Academy Street, Inverness
Tel (01463) 224000 or Edinburgh (Head Office) (0131) 556 2244
Open 1 May to 3 October
Open-top bus tour of Inverness (visit to Culloden Moor is optional), complete with on-board commentary. Passengers picked up and dropped off at various points, including the Farraline Park bus station on Margaret Street, every 45 minutes (C2). Bus ticket offers discounts on admission charges for Culloden Visitor Centre, both Monster centres at Drumnadrochit (Loch Ness), Waltzing Waters (Newtonmore), the Cromarty Courthouse, Highland Music Centre and Balnain House.

HIGHLAND HERITAGE

Tannach Farmhouse, Leanach, Culloden Moor, Inverness
Tel (01463) 798618
Open April to October
Small party day excursions by minibus from Inverness to the Isle of Skye, Glen Affric, Loch Ness and the Speyside Whisky Trail.

INVERNESS TERROR TOUR
Tel (07771) 768652

Open All year
A tour and commentary on terrifying true tales of Inverness and Scotland's horrific past. Leaves from outside Tourist Information Centre at Castle Wynd, Inverness (C3).

JACOBITE CRUISES

Tomnahurich Bridge, Glenurquhart Road, Inverness
Tel (01463) 233999
Fax (01463) 710188
E-mail jacobite@cali.co.uk
Open April to October
Credit/debit cards accepted, private parking, liquor licence. Morning and afternoon cruises on the Caledonian Canal and Loch Ness. Coach and cruise trips visiting Urquhart Castle and the Monster Exhibition Centre. Light refreshments and a bar are available on board. Courtesy transport is available from Inverness Tourist Office 20 minutes before sailing. Booking is recommended during high season. Only round trips are suitable for the disabled. Commended by the Scottish Tourist Board.

JOHNSTONE CHAUFFEUR DRIVE

71 Braeside Park, Balloch, Inverness
Tel (01463) 798372

Fax (01463) 790179
Driver/guide tours for
individuals and small groups
of up to six people, whether a
day in the Highlands or
several days throughout
Scotland.

KEN WHITE'S GUIDED
WALKS
251 Drumossie Avenue,
Inverness
Tel (01463) 223168
A guided walk taking in the
scenic and historic sights of
Inverness. Summer months
daily. Winter months by
arrangement.

LOCH NESS COACH AND
BOAT TOUR
Inverness Traction, 6 Burnett
Road, Longman, Inverness
Tel (01463) 239292
Fax (01463) 712338
Daily coach and boat trips to
Loch Ness, open-top bus
tours. Local bus services.
Three tours are on offer (1)
the Full Day Grand Tour; (2)
the Half-day Grand Tour; (3)
the Evening Loch Ness Tour,
as well as tours to Culloden
and north-west Sutherland.

MACAULEY CHARTERS
Mealishal, Dores, Inverness-
shire IV1 2TR
Tel (01463) 717337
Fax (01463) 751263

Open May to October
An environmentally friendly
tour to see dolphins, seals and
birdlife in the Moray Firth.

MORAY FIRTH CRUISES
Shore Street Quay,
Shore Street, Inverness
Tel (01463) 717900
Fax (01463) 717900
E-mail morayfirth.cruise@
virgin.net
Open March to October
These dolphin and scenic
cruises are one of the main
attractions in the Highlands.
The *Miss Serenity*, carries 90
passengers in comfort with a
high standard of safety. Light
refreshments and snacks. Only
a five-minute walk from the
tourist office and town centre.
Courtesy transport available.

NESSIE BACKPACKERS
Shore Street, Beauly,
Inverness-shire IV4 7DB
Tel (01463) 783111
Offering two coach tours
around the Highlands: Two-
day 'Highland Romp', which
includes various stop-off
points at Loch Ness, Eilean
Donan Castle, Kyle of
Lochalsh (home of TV's
Hamish Macbeth), Torridon
mountain range, Beauly
village and priory, then back
to Inverness; three-day Skye
and West Highlands tour

includes a ferry to the Isle of Skye, Dunvegan Castle, Mallaig, Glenfinnan and Fort William, views of Ben Nevis, then returns to Inverness.

WINDROSE CRUISES
7 Beresford Court,
101 East Trinity Road,
Edinburgh, EH5 3EX
Tel (0131) 551 2233

Fax (0131) 551 2233
Open February to December
Skipper/charter cruises of the Great Glen and the West Coast. On-shore accommodation and allied activities. Also available are individual cruises specially tailored to customers' requirements.

CYCLING AND MOTORCYCLING HOLIDAYS

HIGHLAND MOTORCYCLE HOLIDAYS
16 Beechwood Road,
Raigmore, Inverness
Tel (01463) 242025
Open May to October
Website www.merkinch.org.uk/hmch
Bookings taken for bed and breakfast camp for motorcycles. Touring base for three to four nights and two to three days. Help available with *en-route* and departure accommodation.

SCOTTISH CYCLING HOLIDAYS
87 Perth Street, Blairgowrie, Perthshire
Tel (01250) 876100
Fax (01250) 873383
Open All year
Specialists in self-led, group and tailor-made tours in the Highlands and Islands. Accommodation, transfers, luggage carried, cycle hire.

TRANSPORT

TAXIS AND CHAUFFEUR SERVICES

CULLODEN TAXIS
Culloden Service Station,
Barnchurch Road, Culloden
Tel (01463) 790000
Fax (01463) 794555

RANK RADIO TAXIS
111 Academy Street, Inverness
Tel (01463) 221111/220222
Fax (01463) 220303

SEEMORE SAFARIS
Dunbar Cottage, 31 High
Street, Nairn
Tel (01667) 454535
Escorted tours of the
Highlands by land or sea.

TARTAN TAXIS
Old Filling Station,
Drumrossie, Inverness
Tel (01463) 233033

BICYCLE HIRE

BARNEY'S BICYCLE HIRE
Barney's Newsagents, 35
Castle Street, Inverness
Tel (01463) 232249
Open April to October,

9 a.m. to 9 p.m.
Daily mountain-bike hire
from £7. Explore the
Highlands at your leisure.
New bikes acquired yearly.

CAR HIRE

ARNOLD CLARK HIRE DRIVE
Citroën Complex, 47-49
Harbour Road, Inverness
IV1 1VF
Tel (01463) 236200
Fax (01463) 715329

AUTO SHUTTLE EXPRESS LTD
The Gate House, Knowle
House, Cranleigh, Surrey,

GU6 8RD
Tel (0990) 502309
Fax (01483) 268866
Car transportation to and
from Scotland. Destinations
include Glasgow, Edinburgh,
Inverness, Aberdeen,
departing from the south-east.

AVIS RENT A CAR LTD
Inverness (Dalcross) Airport,

Inverness IV2 2JB
Tel (01677) 462787
Fax (01677) 462837
Open All year
Special weekly and weekend
rates. Delivery services and
one-way rentals available.

BUDGET RENT A CAR
Railway Terrace, Inverness
IV1 1NW
Tel (01463) 713333
Fax (01463) 713185
Car and van rental.

EUROPCAR
Millburn Road, Inverness
IV12 5BE
Tel (01463) 235337
Fax (01463) 234886
A free meet-and-greet service
at Inverness airport.

H.W. JACK (CAR HIRE) LTD
17 Henderson Drive,
Inverness IV1 1TR
Tel (01463) 236572
Fax (01463) 236544

KEN'S GARAGE (RENTAL)
15b Harbour Road, Longman
Industrial Estate, Inverness
IV1 1SY
Tel (01463) 717606
Fax (01463) 717626

KENNING CAR & VAN RENTAL
Unit 3, Highland House,
Longman Road, Inverness
IV1 1RY

Tel (01463) 242400
Fax (01463) 242400
Car, van and minibus rental.
Local and one-way service
available. All inclusive rates.

NATIONAL CAR RENTAL
Shore Street, Inverness IV1
1NG
Tel (01463) 238084
Fax (01463) 719904
Special holiday rates. One way
available. Free delivery in town.

SHARP'S RELIABLE WRECKS
Highland Rail House, Station
Square, Academy Street,
Inverness IV1 1LE
Tel (01463) 236684/236694
Fax (01463) 713777
Includes free after-hours and
weekend service. A family-
run, self-drive rental firm
established in 1978.

THRIFTY CAR HIRE
33 Harbour Road, Inverness
IV1 1UG
Tel (01463) 224466
Fax (01463) 711999
Cars, vans, MPVs and 4x4s.
Local delivery. Pick-up at
airport, bus and train stations.

VOLKSWAGEN RENTAL
Hawco, Harbour Road,
Inverness IV1 1VF
Tel (01463) 236111
Fax (01463) 710327

CAR BREAKDOWN AND RECOVERY

CAR TUNING & SERVICING
28 Seafield Road, Inverness
Tel (01463) 712424

MACRAE & DICK LTD
Harbour Road, Inverness
Tel (01463) 716716
For all makes of car.

SHOPS AND STORES

BABY GOODS

BOBTAILS BABY EQUIPMENT HIRE
Inverness IV1 1ST
Tel (01463) 242123
Bobtails hire out backpacks, lightweight buggies, car seats, travel cots and lots more. They can deliver direct to your hotel and offer daily hire. 11 Lotland Street (see Shore Street, B1), follow Shore Street, away from town centre, follow on to Cromwell Road, take second right turning on to Lotland Street.

BOOKSHOPS

BOOKWORLD
Tel (01463) 713910
Unit 36, Eastgate Shopping Centre (C2)

CELTIC SPIRIT
Tel (01463) 714796
14 Church Street (C2)
Metaphysical bookshop; gifts and alternative therapies.

CHRISTIAN LITERATURE CRUSADE
Tel (01463) 238876
98a Church Street (C3)

JAMES THIN LTD
Tel (01463) 233500
29 Union Street (C2)

JOHN MENZIES
Tel (01463) 233885
25-33 High Street (C3)

LEAKEY'S SECONDHAND BOOKSHOP
Tel (01463) 239947
Church Street (C2)
The largest second-hand bookshop in Scotland, Leakey's offers a constantly changing stock of books, prints and maps.

WATERSTONE'S BOOKSELLERS
Tel (01463) 717474
50-52 High Street (C3)

WESLEY OWEN BOOKS AND MUSIC
Tel (01463) 226152
23 Castle Street (C3)

CHEMISTS AND DRUG STORES

BOOTS THE CHEMIST
Tel (01463) 225167
Eastgate Shopping Centre
(C2)

FORBES C.S. MERKINCH
PHARMACY
Tel (01463) 232217
54 Grant Street (B1)

LLOYD'S PHARMACY
Tel (01463) 233208
10 Church Street (C2)

LLOYD'S PHARMACY
Tel (01463) 233545

8 Greig Street (off Kenneth
Street) (B3)

MOSS CHEMISTS
Tel (01463) 231192
2 Southside Road (C4/C5)

SEMICHEM
Tel (01463) 239608
27 Queensgate (C2)

SUPERDRUG
Tel (01463) 232587
12 High Street (C3)

CLOTHES (LADIES)

CHARLES MORGAN
Tel (01463) 224697
110 Church Street (C2)

COUNTRY CASUALS
Tel (01463) 224727
7-17 Union Street (C2)

DOROTHY PERKINS
Tel (01463) 241621
23 Eastgate Shopping Centre
(C2)

ETAM
Tel (01463) 241687
53 High Street (C3)

EVANS
Tel (01463) 242110/237170
28 Eastgate Shopping Centre
(C2)

MACKAY'S
Tel (01463) 241066
42 Academy Street (C2)

MONSOON
Tel (01463) 235365
24 Eastgate Shopping Centre
(C2)

NEXT
Tel (01463) 233590
32 Eastgate Shopping Centre
(C2)

OASIS
Tel (01463) 224024
23 High Street (C3)

PATRICIA
Tel (01463) 715635
7–9 Queensgate Arcade (C2)

PRINCIPLES
Tel (01463) 224883
27 Eastgate Shopping Centre
(C2)

TOP SHOP
Tel (01463) 242494
13-14 Eastgate Shopping
Centre (C2)

RIVER ISLAND
Tel (01463) 231350
18 Eastgate Shopping Centre
(C2)

WALLIS
Tel (01463) 714630
30 Eastgate Shopping Centre
(C2)

SIGNATURE BY FIONA
MACDONALD
Tel (01463) 238335
36 Eastgate (C3)

CLOTHES (MEN)

BURTON MENSWEAR
Tel (01463) 232278
39 High Street (C3)

PAT J. MACKENZIE
Tel (01463) 715795
1 Queensgate (C2)

THE FACTORY SHOP
Tel (01463) 712307
19 Lombard Street (C3)

PETER GREEN
Tel (01463) 220142
31 Church Street (C2)

JEANSTER
Tel (01463) 710989
37 Eastgate Shopping Centre
(C2)

TOP MAN
Tel (01463) 242502
12 Eastgate Shopping Centre
(C2)

MAX CLOTHING
Tel (01463) 223869
10 Drummond Street
(C3/C2)

L'UOMO
Tel (01463) 713411
22 Baron Taylor's Street
(C3/C2)

CLOTHES (SCOTTISH TRADITIONAL)

CHISHOLM'S HIGHLAND DRESS
Tel (01463) 234599
Fax (01463) 223009
47-51 Castle Street (C3)
Hand-made quality kilts, skirts, Highland dress, Scottish gifts and Highland materials.

HECTOR RUSSELL
Tel (01463) 222781
Fax (01463) 713414
4-9 Huntly Street (B2)
Kiltmakers and retailers of the finest Scottish gifts. Kiltmaking visitor centre. Commended by the Scottish Tourist Board.

DELICATESSENS

THE GOURMET'S LAIR
Tel (01463) 225151
8 Union Street (C2)

DEPARTMENT STORES

ARNOTTS
Tel (01463) 23661
7 Union Street (C2)

MARKS & SPENCER
Tel (01463) 224844
9 Eastgate (C3)

C&A
Tel (01463) 713300
Eastgate Shopping Centre (C2)

WOOLWORTHS
Tel (01463) 238483/231684
13-15 High Street (C3)

LITTLEWOOD
Tel (01463) 236626
Bridge Street (C3)

DRY CLEANERS

COPPERFIELD CLEANERS
Tel (01463) 715070
58 Church Street (C2)
Suede and leather specialists.

MUNRO CLEANERS
Tel (01463) 232165
34 Baron Taylor's Street (C3/C2)

JOHNSONS THE CLEANERS
Tel (01463) 220374
59 Academy Street (C2)

GENERAL AND CONVENIENCE STORES

BARNEY'S
Tel (01463) 232249
35 Castle Street (C3)

CHALKY'S
Tel (01463) 233686
65 Haugh Road (C4)

CHRISTIE'S
Tel (01463) 224812
4 Drummond Street (C3/C2)

DALNEIGH STORES
Tel (01463) 234118
36 St Margaret's Road (A4)

D. LAIDLAW
Tel (01463) 234018
95 Bruce Gardens (A4)

DRUMMOND STORES
Tel (01463) 231275
114 Culduthel Road (C4)

FAIRFIELD STORES
Tel (01463) 715439
40 Montague Row (B3)

HIGHLAND EURO-ASIAN
FOODSTORE
Tel (01463) 714774

32 Kenneth Street (B2/B3)

INVERNESS MINI-MART
Tel (01463) 236341
118 Benula Road (A1)

LA FOODCENTRE
Tel (01463) 233937
36 Laurel Avenue (A4/A3)

MABUHAY (ORIENTAL
SUPPLIES)
Tel (01463) 233935
Academy Street (C2)

MERKINCH STORES
Tel (01463) 232589
1-3 Lochalsh Road (A2)

MUIRTOWN STORES
Tel (01463) 242526
89-91 Telford Street (A2)

SCOTTISH CO-OP
Tel (01463) 230673
59 Church Street (C2)

GIFT SHOPS

ALLSORTS
Tel (01463) 715536
67 Church Street (C2)

CABERFEIDH BAGPIPE SUPPLIES
Tel (01463) 239869
40 Huntly Street (B2)

THE FAMILIAR
Tel (01463) 224838
18 Church Street (C2)

THE HOUSE
Tel (01463) 243117
17 Huntly Street (B2)

PENTANGLE
Tel (01463) 239704
40 Baron Taylor's Street (C3/C2)

SIMPLY SCOTTISH SHOP
Tel (01463) 710960
43 Castle Street (C3)

VICTORIAN GIFT SHOP
Tel (01463) 233430
3 Academy Street (C2)

HAIRDRESSERS AND BARBERS

BARBER SHOP
Tel (01463) 233393
Railway Station (C2)

CAROL ANN HAIRDRESSERS
Tel (01463) 241694
4 Greig Street, off Kenneth Street (B3)

THE HAIR SHOP
Tel (01463) 710112
92 Academy Street (C2)

THE HEAD GARDENER
Tel (01463) 222861
58 Church Street (C3)
Incorporating body care, skin and body clinic.

LESLIE (PROFESSIONAL HAIRDRESSING)
Tel (01463) 231267/234444
8 Eastgate (C3)

RALPH CROOK
Tel (01463) 714771
103 Castle Street (C3)

RD.'S UNISEX HAIR & BEAUTY SALON
Tel (01463) 231091/232762
25 Union Street (B2)

LUGGAGE AND BAG RETAILERS/REPAIRS

GULLIVER'S
Tel (01463) 237662
High Street (– C3)

NEWSAGENTS

BARNEY'S
Tel (01463) 232249
35 Castle Street (C3)

FOX'S
Tel (01463) 232594
47 Tomnahurich Street (B3)

GEORGE S. RODGERS
Tel (01463) 231053
18 Grant Street (B1)

GREIG STREET STORES
Tel (01463) 222883
19 Greig Street, off Kenneth
Street (B3)

JOHN MENZIES
Tel (01463) 222756
Academy Street (C2)

KINGSMILLS GENERAL STORE
Tel (01463) 232026
13 Kingsmills Road (D3)

MACDONALD'S
NEWSAGENTS
Tel (01463) 242516
44 Grant Street (B1)

R.S. MCCOLL
Tel (01463) 714931
23 Queensgate (C2)

MUNRO'S
Tel (01463) 231420
Academy Street (C2)

OPTICIANS

BOOTS OPTICIANS
Tel (01463) 713673
16-28 Eastgate (C3)

DOLLOND & AITCHISON
Tel (01463) 230839
17-19 High Street (C3)

VISION EXPRESS
Tel (01463) 715437
31 Eastgate Centre (C2/D2)

RECORDS, TAPES AND CDS

DR RECORDS
Tel (01463) 236528
3 Market Brae (C3)

THE RECORD RENDEZVOUS
Tel (01463) 231219
14a Church Street (C2)

OUR PRICE
Tel (01463) 225020
21 Eastgate Centre (C2/D2)

SPORTS/OUTDOORS/WALKING SHOPS

CLIVE ROWLAND OUTDOOR SPORTS
Tel (01463) 238746
9 Bridge Street (C3)
Specialist equipment for hill-walking, camping, rock and ice climbing, backpacking, skiing and snow-boarding.

HIGHLAND OUTDOOR
Tel (01463) 236406
73 Castle Street (C3)
Tents, sleepmats, rucksacks, maps, sunglasses, surfwear, boots, hats, socks, breeches, water bottles, waterproofs, map and cases.

SUPERMARKETS

CO-OP
Tel (01463) 711500
Telford street (A2)

TESCO STORES LTD
Tel (01463) 888400
8 Tomnahurich Street (B3)

SAFEWAY STORES
Tel (01463) 713250/713256
Rose Street (C2)

SPORTS AND ACTIVITIES

BOAT HIRE
CALEY CRUISERS
Tel (01463) 236328   *Fax* (01463) 714879
Open March to October
See Telford Street (A2). Follow Telford Street over Muirtown
   Bridge, which spans the Caledonian Canal, turn left on to
   Canal Road.
   Motorboat hire on Loch Ness and the Caledonian Canal.
   No experience necessary as full instruction provided free of
   charge.

BOWLING ALLEYS
ROLLER BOWL
Tel (01463) 235100
167 Culduthel Road (C4)
Twenty-four lanes. All-day licence. Full meals all day.

FISHING
FARRAR FISHING
Culligran Estate, Glen Strathfarrar, Struy, Beauly, Inverness-shire
   IV4 7JZ
Tel (01463) 761285   *Fax* (01463) 761285
Open April to 15 October
Salmon/trout fishing (fly) on river Farr and River Glass by daily
   permit (Beauly catchment). Please phone, fax or write for
   details.

FISHING SCOTLAND (FISHING SCHOOL)
Roy Bridge, Inverness-shire PH31 4AG
Tel (01397) 712812   *Fax* (01397) 712812
E-mail info@fishing-scotland.co.uk
Website www.fishing-scotland.co.uk
Open January to November – pre-reservation essential

Learn to cast a fly for brown trout and rainbow trout at select Highland lochs. Fishing tackle included. Private and small group excursions. Salmon fishing. Please phone, fax or write for details.

GOLF COURSES
INVERNESS GOLF CLUB
Culcabock Road, Inverness
Tel (01463) 231989/239882/233422/233259
See Damfield Road (D4/E4). Continue on to Culcabock Road – car park and clubhouse are on the right.

LOCH NESS GOLF COURSE
Castle Heather Golf Club, Castle Heather, Inverness
Tel (01463) 713335/712695
Eighteen-hole championship golf course and driving range. Trolleys and buggies for hire. Visitors and parties welcome. Bar and restaurant – snacks served all day. Open to the public all year, seven days a week. Phone for directions

TORVEAN GOLF COURSE
Tel (01463) 711434   *Fax* (01463) 712850
Open All year. Eighteen-hole municipal course on A82, two miles from tourist centre.
Glenurquhart Road (A5)

ICE RINKS
INVERNESS ICE CENTRE
Tel (01463) 235711
Bught Park (A6)

LEISURE CENTRES
INVERNESS AQUADOME
Tel (01463) 667500   *Fax* (01463) 667535
Open All year.
Bught Park (A6)
Commended by the Scottish Tourist Board.

INVERNESS SPORTS CENTRE
Tel (01463) 667505   *Fax* (01463) 714494

Open All year.
Bught Park (A6)
Top-class modern indoor sports facility catering for major sports and leisure activities. Adjoining Inverness Aquadome and the Queen's Park Athletics Stadium. Commended by the Scottish Tourist Board.

STADIUM

INVERNESS CALEDONIAN THISTLE FC

Caledonian Stadium, Stadium Road, East Longman, Inverness
Tel (01463) 222880
See Longman Road (C1), continue along Longman Road, past the ring road, past the second ring road, continue on to Stadium Road and follow the road round to the left.

PART 3: THE LOCH NESS VILLAGES

AROUND LOCH NESS

Although the Loch Ness monster mystery certainly boosted tourism to the area when it achieved national media publicity in the 1930s, the thing that immediately occurs to visitors touring the area is that – monster or no monster – Loch Ness and the Great Glen would eventually have been just as popular even with no mystery tagged to it.

THE GREAT GLEN
The Great Glen (also known as Glen Albyn or Glen More) is noticeable on even the sketchiest map of Britain. It was caused by a fracture in the earth's core as the tectonic plates veered sideways, carving out a massive fissure and fault line right across the Highlands – almost cutting Scotland in half in the process! The fault line itself continues under the sea towards Northern Ireland, and it is still regarded as the most active earthquake zone in Britain. The Glen is connected to the sea at both ends from the Moray Firth at Inverness, along the River Ness towards Loch Ness, joining the River Oich, Loch Oich, River Lochy, Loch Lochy, Loch Linnhe and Fort William.

THE CALEDONIAN CANAL
The canal, which runs the total length of the Great Glen, was begun in 1804 and took 18 years to complete, and much change was required. The River Oich was moved to one side to allow the canal to run its course, and Lochs Ness and Lochy had to be dammed in order to raise the water levels by one and a half metres to accommodate the lock system on the canal. Many problems were encountered and overcome by the architect of the project – celebrated engineer Thomas Telford – before its completion in 1822. All in all, 35 kilometres of waterway had to be excavated to accommodate the canal. It makes one wonder how Telford ever found time to design and build the various bridges and other features which are so prevalent in the area!

The canal proved to be one of the great engineering feats of its day, originally built to allow passenger and cargo ships from Liverpool and Glasgow to navigate a shorter and less hazardous route to the port of Inverness. However, the busy traffic never quite peaked along the canal, although fishing boats still follow this course between east and west coasts, while barges, cruises and yachts regularly negotiate the lock system which Telford lovingly constructed all those years ago.

VISITING LOCH NESS

There are two ways to explore Loch Ness from Inverness. Take the busy trunk road (A82) on the north shore, which joins the loch at the aptly named Lochend and hugs the shoreline until reaching Fort Augustus at its southern tip – with the exception of villages Drumnadrochit and Invermoriston, which jut inland away from the lochside. Alternatively, you may prefer the more quiet and no less scenic south shore route, so follow the signs for Dores along the B862 and, on reaching Dores, either follow the shoreline along the B852 to Inverfarigaig and Foyers, or stay on the B862 to skirt smaller lochs, gaining a bird's-eye view of Loch Ness, to Whitefield, Torness, Gortheck and Errogie, joining the B852 at Stratherrick.

Drumnadrochit and Lewiston are separate villages, though are only one mile apart, so I have included them together.

Glenmoriston, as the name suggests, is the name of the glen – with Invermoriston as the first village of Glenmoriston you reach while driving along the A82, so these two areas I have linked together.

The section on Foyers covers the main village of Upper Foyers on the B852 south shore lochside road, and Lower Foyers, which is reached by a tree-lined road on the right-hand side from Dores, which brings you closer to the loch edge. The two villages generally think of themselves as one and the same, and I have them here together.

See page 59 for details of accommodation listings. Details of bus services linking the Loch Ness villages are given on page 206.

ABRIACHAN

SELF-CATERING ACCOMMODATION

ACHABUIE HOLIDAYS

Achabuie, Abriachan, Inverness IV3 6LE

Tel (01463) 861285

Open April to October

Property 1 house, 3 bedrooms, sleeps 6.

Prices £200–£375 per week.

STB rating Self-catering **

BALBEG MILL

Denwick House, Denwick, Alnwick, Northumberland NE66 3RE

Tel (01665) 605865

Open All year

Property 1 cottage, 3 bedrooms, sleeps 6.

Prices £215–£450 per week.

Comments Situated in the hills with outstanding views towards Loch Ness, this charmingly restored cornmill is set in grounds of five acres, bordered by a mill stream. Very well equipped and delightfully furnished. Inverness ten miles; riding and sailing nearby; private loch fishing.

STB rating Self-catering ****

MRS K. FORSTER

Lochlait, Abriachan, Inverness IV3 6LB

Tel (01463) 861215

Open All year

Property 1 caravan, 2 bedrooms, sleeps 4.

Prices £120–£150 per week

STB rating Award pending.

Purlie Lodge, Abriachan, Inverness IV3 6LE
Tel (01463) 861295
Open All year
Property 2 apartments, 1 bedroom, sleeps 2.
Prices £165–£195 per week.
STB rating Self-catering ***

IDEAS FOR DAYS OUT
ABRIACHAN NURSERIES
Lochness Side, Inverness IV3 6LA
Tel (01463) 861232   *Fax* (01463) 861232
Open February to November, 9 a.m. to 7 p.m. (or dusk)
Outstanding garden and nursery on Loch Ness. Mail order
    available. Commended by the Scottish Tourist Board.

BRACKLA

HOTELS
THE CLANSMAN HOTEL
Brackla, Loch Ness-side, Inverness IV3 6LA
Tel (01456) 450236 *Fax* (01456) 450845
Open April to October
Rooms 28, all en-suite (single and double)
Prices Single – April, May, June, £25; July, August, September, £35; October, £25. Double – April, May, June, £49; July, August, September, £59; October, £49.
Facilities Colour TV; tea/coffee-making facilities; direct-dial telephones; baby-listening devices in all rooms.
Comments The only hotel situated in its own grounds on the shores of Loch Ness. Includes a spacious observation lounge bar and dining-room which have panoramic views over Loch Ness and the hills beyond. Bar meals and afternoon teas; Scottish seasonal entertainment; gift shop; entertainment; games room with video recorder etc.
STB rating Hotel ***

SELF-CATERING ACCOMMODATION
LOCH NESS SELF-CATERING FLATS
(See Clansman Hotel above)
Flat 1 2 double bedrooms and 1 bedroom with bunk beds.
Price £390 per week.
Flat 2 1 double bedroom with 2 single beds.
Price £350 per week.
Facilities Ample private parking facilities; colour TV; microwave; washer-dryer; refrigerator plus a safe fenced-in garden area and occupants are welcome to use the hotel's facilities. Nine miles from Inverness – three miles from Drumnadrochit.
Stays of less than one week are available.

DORES

While Drumnadrochit is perhaps the tourist centre for Loch Ness and Fort Augustus the boat enthusiasts' entrance into Loch Ness via the Caledonian Canal, the village of Dores is my personal favourite. It is larger than a hamlet, so you won't miss it if you happen to blink at the wrong time, but it is also set on the quieter south shore – the first village on the B862 from Inverness.

The centre of the village is certainly the Dores Inn, opposite the residential area, nestling just on the brink of Loch Ness and the pretty grey-pebbled beach which stretches off into the distance. A favourite weekend haunt for Invernessians, this village has an interesting history and the local schoolchildren have prepared an itinerary in the form of a leaflet which can be purchased from the Dores Inn.

More often than not, you will see Steve Feltham and his mobile home displaying the emblem 'Nessie-Serry Independent Research' because Dores is also his favourite spot.

THE DORES INN
Dores Road, Loch Ness
Tel (01463) 741203
Open All day in summer; 11 a.m. to 3 p.m. and 5 p.m. in winter
  Meals available 6 p.m. to 8 p.m. seven days and open for snacks (toasties, pastries, scones, jam, shortbread, tea and coffee) in the preceding hours.

You have a choice of routes from Dores
1. Stay on the B862 which winds up the hill, skirting smaller lochs such as Duntelchaig, Ceo Glais, Tarff and the larger Loch Mohr (connected to Loch Ness for the hydroelectric pumping station at Lower Foyers), and leading to Whitebridge, Gorthleck, Errogie and Torness and offering aerial views of Loch Ness.
2. Continue on to the B851, which passes Inverfarigaig and its

forest trail, Foyers and the turn-off to Lower Foyers. (The ten miles between Dores and Foyers skirts the lochside, and although the road is narrow it offers regular 'passing places' to ensure a safe journey for motorists and there are a number of specially built picnic points with steps leading down to the lochside.) After Foyers the road climbs up the hillside to join the B862, which then leads to Whitebridge, Suidhe Chuimen (a viewpoint offering spectacular views over Stratherrick – the highest point of General Wade's military road that connected Fort Augustus with Fort George) and then heads off down to the village of Fort Augustus on the extreme southern tip of Loch Ness.

BED AND BREAKFAST

BEINNDHEARG

Torr Gardens, Dores, Loch Ness, Inverness IV1 2TS

Tel (01463) 751336   *Fax* (01463) 751362

Open All year

Rooms 1 double, 1 twin, 1 family, all rooms are en-suite.

Prices B&B – double/twin, £17–£21

Ver TV in room; tea/coffee facilities; non-smoking; private parking; pay phone available; use of lounge and iron.

Non-ver Use of baby's cot and clothes-drying facilities.

Comments Family-run B&B located in a quiet village 100 metres from Loch Ness, eight miles from Inverness. Ideal base for touring the Highlands. Enjoy lovely walks by the loch, fishing, birdwatching, visit distilleries, local inn with traditional Scottish dishes. Ample parking.

STB rating B&B ***

SELF-CATERING ACCOMMODATION

LOCH NESS LOG CABINS

Drummond, Dores, Inverness IV1 2TX

Tel (01463) 751251   *Fax* (01463) 751240

Open All year

Property 3 log cabins, 2 bedrooms, sleeps 4–6.

Prices £175–£370 per week

Directions Turn left at Dores junction and continue on the B862 for two miles. Loch Ness Log Cabins is on the right-hand side.

STB rating Self-catering *

MR G. & MRS M. FINLAY
Ness Cottage, Dores, by Inverness IV2 6TR
Tel (01463) 751298
Open All year
Property 1 apartment, 3 bedrooms, sleeps 2–7
Prices £250–£350 per week
STB rating Self-catering ****

SCANIPORT (NEAR DORES)
Tel (01463) 751323
Open All year
Rooms 1 double, 1 twin, 1 room en-suite, 1 room private facility.
Prices B&B – single, £18–£25; B&B plus evening meal, £33–£40
Ver Tea/coffee facilities in room; private parking; use of lounge.
Comments Tranquillity and comfort are offered in this Georgian
    farmhouse just a mile from the shores of Loch Ness and a
    handy ten minutes from Inverness. An ideal base to tour the
    Highlands, local riding, good birdwatching, fishing and
    stalking with scenic walking on the doorstep. Splendid
    breakfasts – and suppers by arrangement. Log fires. Long-stay
    B&B discounted rates by negotiation.
STB rating B&B ****

DRUMNADROCHIT AND LEWISTON

Drumnadrochit is the first main village reached when approaching from Inverness along the A82 trunk road along the northern shore and is often considered to be the natural centre for the area. This is due to the number of local amenities. There are records of a village inn dating from the eighteenth century, though there were settlements here pre-dating this back to ancient times.

Drumnadrochit is the home of two 'monster' centres, often termed rivals – the original visitor centre and the official exhibition centre – both offering documentary film shows on the mystery.

Just below the two visitor centres is an early nineteenth-century bridge built by celebrated engineer Thomas Telford, though it has been widened in recent years to allow heavy traffic to pass over it. The bridge spans the River Enrick as it streams towards the waters of Loch Ness. Passing over the bridge you arrive at the hub of the village, with the village green, before moving on to neighbouring village Lewiston and then on to Urquhart Castle, three miles away.

The edge of the green is dotted with accommodation houses, restaurants and various attractions such as the Drum Farm Play Centre for children and a number of gift shops. The Black Isle Junior Pipe Band perform their music on the green on alternate Wednesdays during the summer months.

Drumnadrochit is also the centre for the Glenurquhart Highland Games, which take place every year on the last Saturday in August, and people travel from right across the Highlands and further afield to join the locals and take part in the festivities.

Like all the villages on the north shore road from Inverness to Fort Augustus, Drumnadrochit is well served by public transport. Like Foyers, Inverfarigaig and Fort Augustus, Drumnadrochit offers a varied selection of public footpaths (from easy walking to strenuous) to explore the area, which is rich in history, commanding good views of Loch Ness and the surrounding countryside.

Drumnadrochit offers many public footpaths to the visitor – local people will know of others – most places of accommodation can offer local information and advice. A helpful booklet, available free of charge from Tourist Information Centres and accommodation places, called *North of the Loch*, details various others. All routes are open to both walkers and cyclists, but not cars or motorbikes.

Above the shop and post office, opposite the village green, stands the bus stop for Inverness and public conveniences – and opposite, by the green, is the bus stop for Urquhart Castle, Invermoriston, Fort Augustus and Fort William. There are two public telephones near the shop. There is a car park and helpful information noticeboard about 200 yards on the right, past the village green on the main road – but overnight stays are not allowed.

TAXIS
Telephone Caroline at DRUMNADROCHIT PRIVATE HIRE on (01456) 450617/450550.
Personal recommendation.

BICYCLE HIRE
Available from FIDDLER'S BAR CAFÉ, Main Street (by the village green), Drumnadrochit IV3 6TX. Tel (01456) 450678.

SHOPS AND STORES
COSTCUTTER
Balmacaan Road, Drumnadrochit
Tel (01456) 450206
Drive through the village, past the residential area on the right, and Costcutter is on the right just before the right turning on to Balmacaan Road and opposite the war memorial. Also incorporates the Fish and Chicken Bar.

DRUMNADROCHIT POST OFFICE
Tel (01456) 450201

The post office is housed at the back of Patterson's General Store, opposite the village green.

BANKS
BANK OF SCOTLAND
High Street, Drumnadrochit
Tel (01456) 450237
Open Monday and Friday, 9.30 a.m. to 12.30 p.m.; Wednesday, 10.30 a.m. to 1 p.m.
Link cash dispenser
Above the main street, between Iceberg Glass and the official Loch Ness Monster Exhibition Centre.

BED AND BREAKFAST
MRS T. BEET
Heatherlea, Balmacaan Road, Drumnadrochit, Inverness-shire IV63 6UR
Tel (01456) 450561
E-mail tjbeet@globalnet.co.uk/
Website www.b-and-b-scotland.co.uk/inverness.htm#Heatherlea
Open April to October
Rooms 1 double, 1 family, 1 en-suite, 1 private facility.
Prices B&B – double/twin from £15.
Ver TV in room; tea/coffee facilities in room; non-smoking; private parking; use of hairdryer and iron.
Non-ver Vegetarian diets available by arrangement; credit/debit cards accepted; use of shower, iron and clothes-drying facilities.
STB rating B&B ****

BRIDGEND HOUSE
The Green, Drumnadrochit, Inverness-shire IV3 6TX
Tel (01456) 450865
Open February to October
Rooms 1 single, 1 double, 1 twin.
Prices B&B – single, £18–£20; double/twin, £18–£20; B&B plus evening meal, £32–£34.
Ver Tea/coffee facilities in room; non-smoking; limited parking; evening meal available; use of lounge; lounge TV and iron.
Comments Centrally located on the edge of the village green,

within very short walking distance of all local amenities.
STB rating B&B **

FERNESS COTTAGE
Glen of Ferness, Lewiston, Drumnadrochit, Inverness-shire
IV3 6WW
Tel (01456) 450564
Open All year
Rooms 2 double/family, 1 twin/family, all rooms en-suite.
Prices B&B – double/twin, £15–£18.
Ver TV in room; tea/coffee facilities in room.
Non-ver Packed lunches available by arrangement; pets welcome
  by arrangement; use of baby's cot and iron.
Comments Fully modernised 200-year-old cottage within walking
  distance of Loch Ness. Ideal touring base for the Highlands.
  Pleasant walks. Glen Affric within easy travelling distance.
STB rating B&B

GLEN ROWAN HOUSE
West Lewiston, Drumnadrochit, Inverness-shire IV3 6UW
Tel (01456) 450235   *Fax* (01456) 450817
E-mail glenrowan@compuserv.com
Open February to November
Rooms 1 double, 2 twin; all rooms en-suite.
Prices B&B – single, £25–£38; double/twin, £16–£22; B&B plus
  evening meal, £26–£32.
Ver TV in room with satellite facility; tea/coffee facilities; non-
  smoking; private parking; pay phone available; use of lounge
  and iron.
Non-ver Credit/debit cards accepted.
STB rating B&B ***

GILLYFLOWERS
Drumnadrochit, Inverness-shire IV3 6UJ
Tel (01456) 450641   *Fax* (01456) 450641
E-mail gillyflower@cali.co.uk,internet
Open All year
Rooms 1 double, 1 twin, 1 en-suite.
Prices B&B – single, £15–£30; double/twin, £13.50–£21.50.
Facilities TV in room; tea/coffee facilities in room; shower; clothes-

drying facilities; vegetarian and special diets catered for.
STB rating B&B ***

KILMORE FARMHOUSE
Drumnadrochit, Inverness-shire
Tel (01456) 450524
Open All year
Rooms 2 double, 1 family, all rooms en-suite.
Prices B&B – double/twin, £15–£18; B&B plus evening meal,
£25–£28.
Ver TV in room; tea/coffee facilities; non-smoking; private
parking; evening meal available; pay phone available; use of
lounge; lounge TV; hairdryer and iron.
Non-ver Packed lunches by arrangement; vegetarian and special
diets available; pets welcome by arrangement; credit/debit cards
accepted; use of baby's cot, iron and clothes-drying facilities.
Comments Modern, luxury, custom-built family-run farmhouse
peacefully situated within walking distance from Loch Ness.
Ideal base for hillwalking and touring the Highlands. Rooms
are ground floor and tastefully decorated. Guest lounge
includes log fire. See the Highland cattle.
STB rating B&B ****

C.C. MACDONALD
Nonearn, Pitkerrald Road, Drumnadrochit, Inverness-shire
Tel (01456) 450396
Open March to October
Rooms 1 double, 1 twin, all rooms en-suite.
Prices B&B – double/twin, £15–£20.
Ver Tea/coffee facilities in room; non-smoking; private parking;
use of lounge; hairdryer and iron.
Non-ver Vegetarian diets available.
STB rating B&B ***

MRS H. MACDONALD
Maes Howe, Walled Garden, Balmacaan, Drumnadrochit,
Inverness-shire IV3 6UP
Tel (01456) 450382
Open March to October
Rooms 1 single, 1 double, 1 twin.

Prices B&B – single, £15; double/twin, £15.
Ver Use of TV in lounge and iron; private parking; non-smoking.
STB rating B&B ****

MRS E. PATERSON
Allanmore Farm, Drumnadrochit, Inverness-shire
Tel (01456) 450247
Open April to October
Rooms 2 double, 1 twin.
Prices B&B – double/twin, £14–£15.
Ver Private parking; use of lounge and lounge TV.
STB rating B&B ***

RIVERBANK BED & BREAKFAST
West Lewiston, Drumnadrochit, Inverness-shire IV3 6UL
Tel (01456) 450274
Open March to October
Rooms 2 double, 1 twin; all rooms en-suite.
Prices B&B – double/twin, £15.50–£17.50.
Ver Tea/coffee facilities in room; private parking; use of lounge.
STB rating B&B **

MRS S.M. SILKE
Westwood, Lower Balmacaan, Drumnadrochit, Inverness-shire
IV3 6UR
Tel (01456) 450826   *Fax* (01456) 450826
Open All year
Rooms 1 double, 1 twin, all rooms en-suite.
Prices B&B – double/twin, £16–£21; B&B plus evening meal,
£28–£33.
Ver Tea/coffee facilities in room; non-smoking; private parking;
use of lounge, lounge TV and iron.
Non-ver Packed lunches by arrangement; vegetarian and special
diets by arrangement; pets welcome by arrangement.
STB rating B&B ***

MRS C. URQUHART
Drumbuie Farm, Loch Ness, Drumnadrochit, Inverness-shire
Tel (01456) 450634   *Fax* (01456) 450595
Rooms 2 double, 1 twin, all en-suite.

Prices B&B – double/twin, £17–£22.

Ver TV in room; tea/coffee facilities in room; non-smoking; private parking; use of lounge; evening meal available.

Non-ver Packed lunches by arrangement; vegetarian and special diets by arrangement; iron and clothes-drying facilities.

Comments A warm welcome awaits you at Drumbuie Livestock Farm, home to the Urquhart family and their herd of Highland cattle. This working farm overlooks Loch Ness, with its stunning views and ever-changing beauty. Luxury farmhouse catering for every need. All rooms are ground floor with en-suite facilities. Four-poster bed available.

STB rating B&B ****

MRS JUDITH WITTY

The Haining, Lower Balmacaan, Drumnadrochit, Inverness-shire IV3 6UR

Tel (01456) 450837

Open April to October

Rooms 2 double, 1 twin, all rooms en-suite.

Prices B&B – double/twin from £16.

Ver TV in room; tea/coffee facilities; limited parking.

STB rating B&B **

WOODLANDS

East Lewiston, Drumnadrochit, Inverness-shire IV3 6UL

Tel (01456) 450356

Website www.net.trak.com/-ecs/guest/woodla/

Open All year

Rooms 2 double, 1 twin; all rooms en-suite.

Ver TV in room; tea/coffee facilities; non-smoking; private parking; evening meal available; pay phone available; use of lounge; hairdryer and iron.

Non-ver Credit/debit cards accepted; use of baby's cot; clothes-drying facilities.

STB rating B&B ***

GUEST HOUSES

CLUNEBEG HOUSE

Clunebeg Estate, Drumnadrochit, By Loch Ness, Inverness-shire IV3 6UU

Tel (01456) 450387   *Fax* (01456) 450854

Open All year

Rooms 2 double, 3 twin, 1 family, all rooms en-suite.

Prices B&B – single, £20–£28; double/twin, £18–£24; B&B plus evening meal, £30–£36.

Ver TV in room; tea/coffee facilities; private parking; evening meal available.

Comments A comfortable, modern, purpose-built lodge on a quiet estate overlooking Drumnadrochit by Loch Ness. All rooms en-suite with TV. Licensed restaurant specialising in the traditional taste of Scotland. Pony trekking and woodland walks in the estate. Forest regeneration scheme.

STB rating Guest House *

A.D. MACDONALD-HAIG

Reservations, Borlum, Drumnadrochit, Inverness-shire IV3 6XN

Tel (01456) 450358   *Fax* (01456) 450358

Website www.ibmcug.co.uk/-ecs/guest/borlum/borlum.html

Open All year

Rooms 4 double, 1 twin, 1 family, 2 rooms en-suite.

Prices B&B – double/twin, £20.50–£23.50.

Ver Use of lounge; lounge TV and iron; non-smoking; private parking; pay phone available.

Non-ver Packed lunches by arrangement; vegetarian and special diets by arrangement; use of baby's cot; credit/debit cards accepted.

STB rating Guest House ***

HOTELS

THE BENLEVA HOTEL

Drumnadrochit, Inverness-shire IV3 6UH

Tel (01456) 450288   *Fax* (01456) 450781

Open All year

Rooms 1 single, 3 double, 3 twin, 2 family, 7 rooms en-suite.

Prices B&B – single, £20–£35; double/twin, £22–£35.

Ver TV in room; tea/coffee facilities; non-smoking; private parking; evening meal available; portage; use of hairdryer.

Non-ver Packed lunches by arrangement; pets welcome by arrangement; credit/debit cards accepted.

Comments Enjoy a relaxing family holiday at this small, family-run hotel close to Loch Ness and an ideal touring base. Well-appointed bedrooms with colour TV and tea-making facilities. The hotel offers a comfortable residents' lounge, a lounge bar and an attractive dining-room offering a choice menu for Highland breakfasts and dinners with a good variety of vegetarian meals.

Points of Interest The Benleva Hotel is reputed to be haunted by the ghost of a former minister of religion. The grounds of the hotel include a tree which is the second largest Spanish sweet chestnut tree in Scotland and, according to local legend, it was the hanging tree where many criminals were executed.

STB rating Hotel **

DRUMNADROCHIT HOTEL

Drumnadrochit, Loch Ness, Inverness-shire IV3 6TU

Tel (01456) 450202   *Fax* (01456) 450793

Open All year

Rooms 3 single, 10 double, 6 family; all rooms en-suite.

Prices B&B – single, £24.50–£47; double/twin, £24.50–£37.

Ver TV in room; tea/coffee facilities in room; telephone in room; non-smoking; limited parking; evening meal available.

Non-ver Packed lunches by arrangement; vegetarian and special diets available; pets welcome by arrangement; credit/debit cards accepted; use of baby's cot and iron.

STB rating Hotel **

GLENURQUHART HOUSE HOTEL

by Drumnadrochit, Inverness-shire IV3 6TJ

Tel (01456) 476234   *Fax* (01456) 276286

Open All year

Rooms 2 double, 2 twin, 3 family; all rooms en-suite.

Prices B&B – single, £30–£50; double/twin, £25–£35; B&B plus evening meal, £40–£65.

Ver TV in room; tea/coffee facilities in room; non-smoking; private parking; evening meal available; portage; laundry service.

STB rating Hotel ***

LOCH NESS LODGE HOTEL
Drumnadrochit, Inverness-shire IV3 6TJ
Tel (01456) 450342   *Fax* (01456) 450429
E-mail donald@lochness-centre.com
Rooms 1 single, 5 double, 21 twin, 3 family; 30 rooms en-suite.
Prices B&B – single, £30–£50; double/twin, £25–£40; B&B plus
    evening meal, £40–£60.
Ver TV in room; tea/coffee facilities in room; telephone in room;
    limited parking; evening meal available; portage; room service;
    laundry service; use of hairdryer.
Non-ver Packed lunches by arrangement; vegetarian and special
    diets available; credit/debit cards accepted; use of baby's cot.
STB rating Hotel **

POLMAILY HOUSE HOTEL
Loch Ness, Drumnadrochit, Inverness-shire IV63 6XT
Tel (01456) 450343   *Fax* (01456) 450813
E-mail polmailyhousehotel@btinternet.com
Open All year
Rooms 2 double, 2 twin, 6 family, all rooms en-suite.
Prices B&B – single, £40–£55; double/twin for two people,
    £80–£130; B&B plus evening meal for two, £130–£160.
Ver TV in room; tea/coffee facilities; telephone in room; private
    parking; non-smoking; evening meal available; room service;
    laundry service; indoor swimming pool; leisure facilities; use of
    hairdryer.
STB rating Hotel ***

HOSTELS
LOCH NESS BACKPACKERS LODGE
Coiltie Farmhouse, East Lewiston, Drumnadrochit IV3 6UJ
Tel (01456) 450807
Open All year
Rooms 6 rooms, 32 beds.
Prices £8.50–£9 per person, per night.

CARAVAN AND CAMPING PARKS

BORLUM FARM CARAVAN AND CAMPING PARK
Drumnadrochit, Inverness-shire IV3 6XN
Tel (01456) 450220   *Fax* (01456) 450358
Open March to October
Pitches 25 touring pitches. £3.90 per adult; £1.95 per child; £1.90
    electric; £1.50 awnings.
STB rating ✔✔✔

SELF-CATERING ACCOMMODATION

ACHMONY HOLIDAYS
Drumnadrochit, by Loch Ness, Inverness IV3 6UX
Tel (01456) 450357   *Fax* (01456) 450830
Open March to November
Property 10 chalets, 3 bedrooms (property sleeps 2–6).
Prices £195–£510 per week.
Comments Enjoy your holiday in an idyllic location above Loch
    Ness. Three-bedroom chalet has fully fitted kitchen, bathroom,
    lounge with CTV and patio door. Ideal central base for touring.
    Drumnadrochit has hotels, shops and boat trips on Loch Ness.
    No pets allowed.
  STB rating Self-catering ****

MISS M.M. BROOK
Lochletter Lodges, Balnain, Drumnadrochit, Inverness-shire IV3
    6TJ
Tel (01456) 476313   *Fax* (01456) 476301
Open March to December
Property 4 chalets, 2–3 bedrooms (property sleeps 4–6).
Prices £160–£410 per week.
STB rating Self-catering ***
Disabled access.

MR R. CODD
Glaichmor, Milton, Drumnadrochit, Inverness-shire IV3 6TZ
Tel (01456) 450257
Open All year
Property 1 chalet, 2 bedrooms (property sleeps 2–5).
Prices £175–£350 per week.
STB rating Self-catering ****

GLENURQUHART LODGES
by Drumnadrochit, Inverness-shire IV3 6TJ
Tel (01456) 476234   *Fax* (01456) 476286
Open All year
Property 5 chalets, 3 bedrooms (property sleeps 6).
Prices £150–£400 per week.
STB rating Self-catering **

MRS C.E. JONES
The Old Barn, Rookery Farm, Back Lane, Pebworth, Warwick-
  shire (property – Drumnadrochit)
Tel (01789) 721534
Open March to October
Property 1 cottage, 3 bedrooms (property sleeps 5–6).
Prices £350–£500 per week.

KILMARTIN CHALET PARK
Glen Urquhart, by Drumnadrochit, Inverness-shire IV3 6TN
Tel (01456) 476371
Open All year
Property 5 chalets, 3 bedrooms (property sleeps 2–7).
Prices £130–£360 per week.
STB rating Self-catering *

LOCH NESS HOLIDAY CARAVANS
Lower Milton Farm, Drumnadrochit, Inverness-shire IV3 6TZ
Tel (01456) 450554   *Fax* (01456) 450554
Open May to September
Property 2 caravans, 2 bedrooms (property sleeps 6).
Prices £120–£165 per week.

LOCH NESS HOLIDAY HOMES
Glen of Ferness, Lewiston, Drumnadrochit, Inverness-shire
  IV3 6UW
Tel (01456) 450564
Open All year
Property 1 house, 1 apartment, 2 bedrooms (property sleeps 2–4).
Prices £150–£350 per week.
STB rating Self-catering **

ROWAN COTTAGE
c/o 7 Harris Road, Inverness IV2 3LS
Tel (01463) 237059   *Fax* (01463) 242092
E-mail elmslie@globalnet.co.uk
Open All year
Property 1 cottage, 3 bedrooms (property sleeps 2–5).
Prices £195–£405 per week.
STB rating Self-catering ****

STRONE HOLIDAY COTTAGES
Loch Ness-side, Drumnadrochit, Inverness-shire IV3 6XL
Tel (01456) 450351   *Fax* (01456) 450351
Open April to September
Property 1 chalet, 2 bungalows (property sleeps 4).
Prices £195–£350 per week.
STB rating Self-catering ***

TORCROFT LODGE
Balnain, Drumnadrochit, Inverness-shire IV3 6TJ
Tel (01456) 476350   *Fax* (01456) 476350
Open March to October plus December/January/Christmas and
    New Year
Property 3 chalets, 2 bedrooms (property sleeps 2–5)
Prices £160–£390 per week.
STB rating Self-catering *** to ****

WHERE TO EAT

FIDDLER'S CAFÉ BAR
Main Street, Drumnadrochit
IV3 6TX
Tel (01456) 450678
Scottish-orientated menu
made from fresh local
produce. Children's menu
available.

THE FISH & CHICKEN BAR
(TAKEAWAY)
Food Market, Balmacaan
Road, Drumnadrochit
Tel (01456) 450123

GLEN SNACK BAR
The (Village) Green,
Drumnadrochit
Tel (01456) 450282

PUBS

LEWISTON ARMS HOTEL
(The Loch Ness Monster
Inn),
Lewiston, Drumnadrochit
Tel (01456) 450225

MOFFAT ARMS
Drumnadrochit

Tel (01456) 450757

SMIDDY BAR
Lewiston, Drumnadrochit
Tel (01456) 450755

ARTS, CRAFTS AND GIFTS

THE ART GALLERY
The Green, Drumnadrochit
Tel (01456) 450695
Open All year
The gallery sells original
paintings by local artists. A
wide choice of souvenirs and
tasteful gifts available.

BITS AND PIECES
Main Street, Drumnadrochit
Tel (01456) 450838

COTTAGE WOODCRAFT
Enrick Cottage, Loch Ness
IV3 6TZ
Tel (01456) 450423
Fax (01456) 450423
Open All year
Directions Take the A831 out
of Drumnadrochit as it turns
off the main street and past
the Original Loch Ness
Monster Exhibition Centre.
Woodturning and country
traditional furniture in native
woods.

ICEBERG GLASS
Victoria Buildings,
Drumnadrochit
Tel (01456) 450601
Open All year
Location Next door to the
Original Loch Ness Monster
Centre, at the top of the main
street.
Glassblowing studio where
you can watch the skilled
glassblowers blow and shape
glass.

THE KEEPER'S COTTAGE
Official Loch Ness Exhibition
Centre
Tel (01456) 450573/ 450202
Fax (01456) 450770
Location Official Loch Ness
Exhibition Centre – the first
building on your right as you
approach Drumnadrochit
from Inverness.

LOCHNESS CLAY WORKS
Bunloit Pottery, Goshem,

Bunloit, Drumnadrochit
Tel (01456) 450402
Open All year
Bright, colourful, practical and playful. After turning off the A82 at Lewiston Bridge, the four-mile journey to the pottery will give you breathtaking views of the majestic Mealfuarvonie. Situated next to an ancient birch forest, 180 metres above Loch Ness, this friendly pottery is run by two colourful lady potters. Their ceramics include soothing oil burners, practical porridge bowls, pretty night lights, unusual teapots and beautiful mugs. Parking available at the pottery.

NESSIE'S NESSESSITIES
Drumnadrochit
Tel (01456) 450800

THE NESSIE SHOP
Drumallan, Drumnadrochit
Tel (01456) 450323

TOURS AND SIGHTSEEING

LOCH NESS CRUISES
The Original Loch Ness Monster Centre, Loch Ness Lodge Hotel, Drumnadrochit
Tel (01456) 450395
Fax (01456) 450785
Open March to October
Hourly cruises on the *Nessie Hunter*. Commentary by local skipper George Edwards. Colour sonar on board. All-weather facilities. Fun for all the family.

LOCH NESS TRAVEL COMPANY
Lewiston, Drumnadrochit
Tel (01456) 450550
Fax (01456) 450550
Car tours, guides and courier services.

IDEAS FOR DAYS OUT

THE BENLEVA WALK

This begins outside the Benleva Hotel on what is locally known as School Lane. To reach this point, pass through the village, turn left on to the first main road before reaching Lewiston, passing the Glenurquhart School, the Benleva Hotel and some bed and breakfast houses (including Gillyflowers), turn right at the cemetery past the waterworks, and climb over two stiles and past a farmer's field to reach the start of the footpath. You will need waterproof boots (preferably wellies) as it involves crossing a stream which is too wide to jump. Although the route is not very well signposted, keep to the River Enrick on your left, then cross the stream and eventually you will reach a point on the shore of Loch Ness within Urquhart Bay offering panoramic views of this quiet part of the loch.

CRAIGMONY

An ancient hill fort with wide-ranging views of Loch Ness. Take the south road straight out of Drumnadrochit, turn right past the bowling club. Take first dirt path on the left where you will see the sign for Craigmony follow on through the gates at the top.

DRUM FARM PLAY CENTRE

The Village Green, Drumnadrochit
Open April to October
Farmyard fun, playbarns, friendly animals, indoor/outdoor play, tearoom and gift shop. Commended by the Scottish Tourist Board.

HIGHLAND RIDING CENTRE

Borlum Farm, Drumnadrochit
Tel (01456) 450220   *Fax* (01456) 450358
Open All year
Directions Drive through Drumnadrochit and Lewiston and you will see a sign for the Borlum Riding Centre.
Overlooking Loch Ness and approved by the BHS, the Borlum Riding Centre is open all year, offering courses for both beginners and experienced riders alike and set in spectacular riding country.

THE JOHN COBB MEMORIAL

The memorial is situated on the left-hand side of the road at Achnahannet, two miles past Urquhart Castle. It is in the form of a beehive cairn and was donated by the people of Glenurquhart to commemorate John Cobb, holder of the land speed record, who died here while attempting to break the world water speed record on 29 September 1952. His boat *Crusader* decelerated after the attempt, seemed to bounce twice and disintegrated on the loch's surface after hitting a patch of turbulence. Although still alive when taken from the wreckage, he was carried up to this hill, where he died just a few metres away from where the memorial now stands. The wording on the memorial reads: 'In memory of a very Gallant Gentleman.' There is also a corresponding memorial to John Cobb on the south shore of the loch between the villages of Dores and Foyers.

Incidentally, Achnahannet was also the site of the former Loch Ness Phenomena Investigation Bureau Ltd, which ran from 1962 to 1972.

THE OFFICIAL LOCH NESS MONSTER EXHIBITION CENTRE

Drumnadrochit

Tel (01456) 450573/450202   *Fax* (01456) 450770

Open All year

Home of the authoritative exhibition on the mysterious phenomenon of Loch Ness (40-minute audio-visual). The exhibition will surprise many people and is aimed at giving tourists an informed view of the mystery and its ongoing investigation. You may or may not agree with the conclusion, but it is well worth a visit. The exhibition presentation was designed, scripted and is narrated by Adrian Shine, leader of the Loch Ness Project, who has appeared on all recent documentaries on the Loch Ness mystery. This recent exhibition was officially opened by renowned explorer and adventurer Sir Ranulph Fiennes on 15 June 1999. Also includes shops, restaurants, crafts, boat trips and a hotel.

THE ORIGINAL LOCH NESS VISITOR CENTRE

Loch Ness Lodge Hotel, Drumnadrochit

Tel (01456) 450218   *Fax* (01456) 450770

Open All year

Professional cinema and exhibition seating 120, with multi-language translations. Gift shops, coffee house. Groups welcome.

URQUHART CASTLE
near Drumnadrochit
Tel (01456) 450551   *Fax* (01456) 450551
Open All year
Directions Drive through Drumnadrochit, pass through Lewiston and past Borlum Farm. Urquhart Castle is on your left.
The remains of one of the largest castles in Scotland. Offers spectacular views of up and down Loch Ness. Limited parking spaces available. Commended by the Scottish Tourist Board.

FORT AUGUSTUS

Although Drumnadrochit is generally considered to be the main village of Loch Ness, Fort Augustus is the largest and certainly one of the prettiest. It seems to have something for everyone.

Until recently, the Fort Augustus Abbey was run by the Benedictine monks, but with their numbers dwindling and despite the number of additional duties they took on for the tourist trade (including the offer of the largest bed and breakfast establishment at Loch Ness), sadly they decided to vacate the premises and it is uncertain what new role the Abbey will play.

Many of the Fort Augustus monks have seen the Loch Ness monster – and they remain some of the most credible eyewitnesses – and for this reason many Nessie enthusiasts have always thought of Fort Augustus Abbey as the central feature on the banks of Loch Ness, the only real equal, perhaps, to Urquhart Castle.

The Caledonian Canal, built by Thomas Telford, is the central feature of Fort Augustus as it runs through the village from the top of the canal locks and then out into Loch Ness. The River Oich also runs into the loch on a parallel with the canal, and you can stand on a jetty and tiny beach positioned between the two and look down the length of the loch.

The Tourist Information Centre, (01320) 366367, and car and coach parks are located on Inverness Road as it turns into Fort Augustus.

BANKS
BANK OF SCOTLAND
Tel (01320) 366297
Open Monday, Thursday and Friday, 9.15 a.m. to 12 noon and
    1.30 p.m. to 4.45 p.m.
Drive straight through the village, take the first right turning past
    the Richmond House Hotel on to Station Road. The Bank of

Scotland is on the left at the top of the road and also houses Bank House Bed and Breakfast.

No cash dispenser here, but there are two located in the village – both of which display the Link logo. One is at the Glen Service Station on Main Street, near the Tourist Information Centre, and the other is outside the post office/A. & W.J. Newsagents, on Canalside.

NEWSAGENTS AND POST OFFICE

A. & W.J., GLEN MOIRA
Canalside, Fort Augustus
Tel (01320) 366373

POST OFFICE
Canalside, Fort Augustus
Tel (01320) 366200
Bureau de Change for
currency transactions.

PETROL STATIONS
THE GLEN (SHELL) SERVICE STATION
Fort Augustus
Tel (01320) 366365

GENERAL STORES
THE MACASKILLS
Canalside, Fort Augustus
Tel (01320) 366207

BED AND BREAKFAST
THE BANK HOUSE
Station Road, Fort Augustus, Inverness-shire PH32 4AX
Tel (01320) 366767

Alan and Mandy Smith had such a love of the Highlands and a keen interest in the Loch Ness mystery that they moved to Scotland and set up their own B&B. Their establishment leans towards Nessie hunters (though is not totally devoted to them) and they possess a good collection of Loch Ness monster videos and a library of books on the subject. They decided against being graded by the STB, though they provide rooms and facilities similar to those offered by STB-registered properties. Please telephone or write for details of rooms, prices and facilities.

Location Drive along Main Street and take the first right turn on to Station Road. Bank House is at the top of the street and is housed in the same building as the Bank of Scotland.

Recommendation (by Rip Hepple, editor of *Nessletter*): 'They are a very nice couple and anyone visiting the area and looking for accommodation could hardly do better than contact them.'

JUNE AND BOB BURNETT
Kettle House, Golf Course Road, Fort Augustus, Inverness-shire PH32 4BY
Tel (01320) 366408
Open February to November
Rooms 2 single, 1 double, 1 twin, 4 en-suite.
Prices B&B – single, £15–£17; double/twin, £15–£17.
Ver TV in room; tea/coffee facilities; non-smoking; private parking; use of lounge and iron.
Non-ver Packed lunches by arrangement; pets welcome by arrangement; use of iron, baby's cot and clothes-drying facilities.
Please telephone or write for details.
STB rating B&B ***

SUE CALLCUTT
Tigh Na Mairi, Canalside, Fort Augustus, Inverness-shire PH32 4BA
Tel (01320) 366766   *Fax* (01320) 366766
Open All year except Christmas and New Year
Rooms 2 double, 1 twin.
Prices B&B – single, £14–£20; double/twin, £11–£18.
Ver TV in room; tea/coffee facilities; non-smoking; private parking; use of lounge; lounge TV.
Non-ver Packed lunches by arrangement; vegetarian and special diets available; use of iron and clothes-drying facilities.
Location At Main Street, looking up towards the top of the canal, follow the road on the right leading to Tigh Na Mairi.
STB rating B&B **

GREYSTONES
Station Road, Fort Augustus, Inverness-shire PH32 4AY
Tel (01320) 366736   *Fax* (01320) 366263
Open All year

Rooms 3 double, 1 twin.

Prices Double/twin, £15–£20.

Location Drive straight through the village, over the level-crossing spanning the canal, and take the first right turning. Greystones is about 100 yards on the right.

MRS M.V. MACLENNAN

Thistle Dubh, Fort Augustus, Inverness-shire PH32 4BN

Tel (01320) 366380

Open March to November

Rooms 2 double, 1 twin; all rooms en-suite.

Prices B&B – single, £20; double/twin, £20.

Ver TV in room; tea/coffee facilities; non-smoking; private parking; use of lounge; lounge TV and iron.

Please telephone or write for details.

MS A.C. MCINNES

Anzac, Auchterawe Road, Fort Augustus, Inverness-shire PH32 4BW

Tel (01320) 366461

Open July to September

Rooms 1 double, 1 twin.

Prices B&B – double/twin, £15–£17.

Ver Tea/coffee facilities; non-smoking; private parking; use of lounge; lounge TV and iron.

Please telephone or write for details.

STB rating **

GORDON AND DOROTHY NAIRN

Appin, Inverness Road, Fort Augustus, Inverness-shire PH32 4DH

Tel (01320) 366541

Open April to September

Rooms 2 double, 1 twin, 2 rooms en-suite, 1 room private facility.

Prices B&B – double/twin, £14–£18.

Ver Tea/coffee facilities in room; non-smoking; private parking; use of lounge and lounge TV.

STB rating B&B **

Cartref, Fort William Road, Fort Augustus, Inverness-shire
   PH32 4BH
Tel (01320) 366255
Open All year
Rooms 2 double, 1 twin, 1 room en-suite, 2 rooms private facility.
Prices B&B – double/twin, £17–£20.
Location Drive along Main Street of Fort Augustus, through the
   village, and take the second right turning on to Fort William
   Road.
STB rating B&B **

MRS L. SERVICE
Sonas, Inverness Road, Fort Augustus, Inverness-shire PH32 4DH
Tel (01320) 366291
Open All year
Rooms 1 double, 1 twin, 1 family, all en-suite.
Prices B&B from £15.
Location See residential area on the left as Inverness Road (A82)
   turns on to Main Street at Fort Augustus, opposite the Tourist
   Information Centre.
STB rating B&B ****

MRS W.H. SEY
Braevard, Main Street, Fort Augustus, Inverness-shire PH32 4BQ
Tel (01320) 366438
Open April to October
Rooms 1 twin, 1 family, all rooms en-suite.
Prices B&B – single, £15–£18; double/twin, £15–£18.
Ver Non-smoking; use of lounge; lounge TV and hairdryer.
Location Main Street, as the name suggests, runs straight through
   the village from Inverness Road on the northern shore of Loch
   Ness (A82) as it winds into the village over the level crossing of
   the Caledonian Canal and joins on to Fort William Road (also
   A82) out of the village.
STB rating B&B ***

GUEST HOUSES
THE BRAE HOTEL
Fort Augustus, Inverness-shire PH32 4DG

Tel (01320) 366289   *Fax* (01320) 366702

Open March to October

Rooms 1 single, 4 double, 2 twin, 6 rooms en-suite, 1 room private
facility.

Prices B&B – single, £32–£35; double/twin, £32–£38.

Ver TV in room; tea/coffee facilities; non-smoking; private
parking; full liquor licence; pay phone available; use of lounge;
lounge TV and iron.

Please ring for directions.

STB rating Guest House ***

HOTELS
CALEDONIAN HOTEL
Fort Augustus, Inverness-shire PH32 4BQ

Tel (01320) 366256   *Fax* (01320) 366629

Open Easter to September

Rooms 1 single, 4 double, 3 twin, 3 family, 7 rooms en-suite.

Prices B&B – single, £20–£37.50; double/twin, £20–£27.50;
B&B plus evening meal, £35–£42.50.

Ver TV in room; tea/coffee facilities; non-smoking; private
parking; evening meal available.

Please ring for directions.

STB rating Hotel **

INCHNACARDOCH LODGE HOTEL
(Overlooking Loch Ness) By Fort Augustus, Inverness-shire
PH32 4BL

Tel (01320) 366258   *Fax* (01320) 366248

Open All year

Rooms 5 double, 4 twin, 4 family, all rooms en-suite.

Ver TV in room; tea/coffee facilities; telephone in room; evening
meal available; limited parking.

Location From Inverness follow Inverness Road (A82) and you
reach the Inchnacardoch Lodge Hotel about half a mile before
reaching Fort Augustus.

STB rating Hotel **

LOVAT ARMS HOTEL
Fort Augustus, Inverness-shire PH32
Tel (01320) 366206   *Fax* (01320) 366677
Open All year
Rooms 4 single, 7 double, 8 twin, 4 family, all rooms en-suite.
Ver TV in room; tea/coffee facilities; telephone in room; non-smoking; private parking; evening meal available.

THE RICHMOND HOUSE HOTEL
Main Street, Fort Augustus
Tel (01320) 366719
Rooms 4 double (2 en-suite), 2 single, 2 twin, 1 family.
Location Drive straight through the village. The Richmond House Hotel is on the row of buildings on your right as you pass the level crossing over the canal.
Please telephone for further details of prices and facilities.

SELF-CATERING ACCOMMODATION
MRS A. MACCORMICK
Torr Dhuin, Auchterawe, Fort Augustus, Inverness-shire PH32 4BT
Tel (01320) 366552
Open All year
Property 1 cottage, 3 bedrooms, sleeps 1–6.
Price £180–£300 per week.
Please write or phone for details.

WHERE TO EAT

CAUSER'S CHIP SHOP (TAKEAWAY)

Tel (01320) 366456

Directions From Main Street at the canal level crossing, looking towards the head of the canal, follow the left road up the hill, running alongside the canal. Causer's Chip Shop is on your left.

THE MOORINGS

Tel (01320) 366484

Directions From the Tourist Information Centre cross the road, turn left on the same side of the canal and walk down the small path. The Moorings is on your left.

Fish and chip restaurant and takeaway. Comfortable seating, friendly service, opposite Fort Augustus Abbey. Lounge window so you can sit and watch the boats sail past into Loch Ness.

THE ROWAN TREE

Tel (01320) 366208

Directions From Main Street at the canal level crossing looking towards the head of the canal, follow the left road running alongside the canal. The Rowan Tree is on your left.

Pizza, pasta, traditional meals such as steak dinners, also scones, baguettes and other snacks served during the day; in the evening the Rowan Tree serves seafood, venison, pheasant.

THE SCOTS KITCHEN

Tel (01320) 366361

Directions Opposite the Tourist Information Centre on Inverness Road.

Very warm welcome from staff serving tea, coffee, snacks and meals.

Meals are also served at the three public houses in Fort Augustus

THE BOTHY
Canalside
Tel (01320) 366710

THE LOCK INN
Canalside
Tel (01320) 366302

RICHMOND HOUSE HOTEL
Main Street
Tel (01320) 366719

IDEAS FOR DAYS OUT

THE CLANSMAN CENTRE

Fort Augustus
Tel (01320) 366444
Open April to September
Seventeenth-century living
history museum and craft
shop. Commended by the
Scottish Tourist Board

Fax (01320) 366221
Open March to January
One-hour cruises aboard the
Royal Scot from the
Caledonian Canal. Includes
the largest sonar on Loch
Ness. 111 seats. Tea, coffee,
beer and spirits available.

CRUISE LOCH NESS

Knockburnie, Fort Augustus
Tel (01320) 366277

GIFT SHOPS

There are a number of gift and souvenir shops, including The
Imray Shop (selling all manner of quality Scottish gifts,
including books and needlecraft) and The Emporium (quality
gifts, including woollen products). Both are on Fort William
Road, just off Canalside. Also The Mill Shop, on the Inverness
Road side of the canal.

SPORTS AND ACTIVITIES

FORT AUGUSTUS GOLF CLUB

Market Hill, Fort Augustus
Tel (01320) 366660

FOYERS

Ten miles from Dores, on the south shore, and two miles after Inverfarigaig, we reach Foyers – home of the Falls of Foyers. The Falls are often described as magnificent and, while the volume of the waterfall has decreased (due to some water being harnessed by the hydroelectric station at Lower Foyers) since Robert Burns wrote a poem about them, they are still a splendid sight.

They can either be approached by a path from the village on the B852 road, just opposite the post office and café, or from the winding road which leads down to Lower Foyers. There are different routes for the paths, but always take care of young children and dogs – the paths can be muddy, particularly in wet weather, and there are some sheer drops along the way, often when you least expect it, though all are signposted and the routes are clearly marked.

The Falls of Foyers path leads to a wooden rail, clinging precariously to the edge overlooking the sheer drop hundreds of feet down.

This is not the only nature trail in the area – there are several ranging from easy-going for families to strenuous for the more adventurous visitor – and I recommend purchasing the leaflet *Paths Around Foyers* from Foyers post office on the main road, produced by the Highland Council Ranger Service. It includes sections on flowers, woodlands, wildlife and nature trails, including the trail at Inverfarigaig. It also includes a detailed map of the whole area, with all facilities marked.

Horse-riders often need permits to follow tracks and some are too steep or impractical on the shorter routes; cyclists are welcome on all roads and vehicle tracks. Wheelchair users will find most routes too steep or rough, though the route to Lower Foyers, including the hydroelectric power station, old pier at Foyers Bay, old bridge and burial ground by Loch Ness are all accessible and worth a visit.

TAXIS

MR AND MRS RULE

Tel (01456) 486234

Mr and Mrs Rule provide a helpful, friendly taxi service. Their motto is 'any distance, any time'.

BED AND BREAKFAST

MRS R.N. GRANT

Intake-House, Foyers, Inverness-shire IV1 2YA

Tel (01456) 486258

Open April to October

Rooms 1 double, 1 twin, 1 room en-suite.

Prices B&B – single, £14–£18; double/twin, £14–£18.

Ver Tea/coffee facilities; non-smoking; private parking; pay phone available; use of lounge; lounge TV; hairdryer and iron.

STB rating B&B ***

GUEST HOUSES

FOYERS BAY HOUSE

Lower Foyers, Inverness IV1 2YB

Tel (01456) 486624   *Fax* (01456) 486337

Open All year

Rooms 3 double, 2 twin, all rooms en-suite.

Prices B&B – double/twin, £22–£27; B&B plus evening meal, £29.50–£39.50.

Ver TV in room; tea/coffee facilities; telephone in room; non-smoking; private parking; evening meal available.

Non-ver Packed lunches by arrangement; credit/debit cards accepted; use of baby's cot and iron.

Location If travelling from Dores and Inverfarigaig, Lower Foyers is reached by taking the right turning down a woodland road, about quarter of a mile before reaching Foyers (also called Upper Foyers).

Comments Victorian villa set in magnificent grounds beside the famous Falls of Foyer overlooking Loch Ness. Conservatory café/restaurant; self-catering lodges within grounds (see self-catering section). An ideal base for touring Loch Ness and the Highlands.

STB rating Guest House **

HOTELS

CRAIGDARROCH HOUSE HOTEL

Foyers, South Loch Ness Side, Inverness-shire IV1 2XU

Tel (01456) 486400   *Fax* (01456) 486444

E-mail davemunro@hotel-loch-ness.co.uk

Website www.hotel-loch-ness.co.uk

Open February to December

Rooms 6 double, 3 twin, 1 family, all rooms en-suite.

Prices B&B – single, £45–£65; double/twin, £45–£65; B&B plus evening meal, £65–£90.

Ver TV in room; tea/coffee facilities; telephone in room; non-smoking; private parking; evening meal available; room service; portage; laundry service; use of hairdryer.

Non-ver Vegetarian and special diets available by arrangement; pets welcome by arrangement; credit/debit cards accepted.

Location Travelling from Dores and Inverfarigaig, the main entrance is from the road to Lower Foyers, taking the first right turning down the wooded lane away from the road, although there is an entrance, also from Foyers (Upper Foyers), on the main road.

STB rating Hotel ****

THE FOYERS HOTEL

Foyers, Loch Ness, Inverness-shire IV1 2XT

Tel (01456) 486216   *Fax* (01456) 486216

Open All year

Rooms 2 single, 5 double, 2 family, 8 rooms en-suite, 1 room private facility.

Prices B&B – single, £35–£45; double/twin, £40–£45.

Ver Tea/coffee facilities in room; non-smoking; private parking; evening meal available; portage; use of hairdryer.

Location About half a mile from the village of Foyers. Restaurant and bar also open to non-residents.

STB rating Hotel ***

SELF-CATERING ACCOMMODATION

ELMBANK APARTMENTS

2 Elmbank, Foyers, Inverness-shire IV1 2YF

Tel (01456) 486610

Open All year

Property 1 apartment, 2 bedrooms, sleeps 4–5.
Prices £100–£230 per week.
STB rating Self-catering **

Lower Foyers, Inverness IV1 2YB
Tel (01456) 486624   *Fax* (01456) 486337
Open All year
Property 6 chalets, 3 bedrooms, sleeps 2–6.
Prices £200–£450 per week.
STB rating Self-catering **

INVERFARIGAIG

Inverfarigaig is a hamlet consisting of a cluster of beautiful white houses at the side of the south shore road as it twists inland towards the village of Foyers two miles further along.

A little way before reaching this point is the signpost 'Inverfarigaig Dun Dearduil' – a network of forest walks, some of which lead up the pass to Loch Mhor on the road above Loch Ness. They offer exhilarating views of Loch Ness and also of the Inverfarigaig Gorge and the site of an ancient hill fort called Dun Dearduil.

The short road leading to the trail is signposted on the B851 south shore road, and a few yards further up is ample parking space at the side of the road and a red telephone box. This point is also used as a bus stop for the scheduled services running from Inverness, Dores and Foyers, then back again.

There is an unstaffed but detailed and helpful visitor centre, describing the aims of the Forestry Enterprise (formerly the Forestry Commission), at the entrance to the Nature Trail, as well as a car park and public conveniences.

TAXIS
MR AND MRS RULE
Tel (01456) 486234 (see page 195)

SELF-CATERING ACCOMMODATION
The only accommodation registered by the Highlands of Scotland Tourist Board in the immediate area is self-catering.

WILDERNESS COTTAGES
Island Cottage, Inverfarigaig, Inverness-shire IV1 2XR
Tel (01456) 486631   *Fax* (01456) 486631
Open All year
Property 3 cottages, 2–3 bedrooms, sleeps 4–6.
Prices £150–£500 per week.
STB rating Self-catering *** to ****

INVERMORISTON AND GLENMORISTON

Following the A82 trunk road along the northern shores of Loch Ness, the next village past Drumnadrochit, Lewiston and Urquhart Castle is Invermoriston.

Four miles before you reach Invermoriston, on the road from Inverness, is the Loch Ness Youth Hostel at Alltsigh, situated on a small beach on the banks of the loch.

LOCH NESS YOUTH HOSTEL

Tel (01320) 351274

Open 3 March to end of October. To make reservations out of season, either leave a message on the above number or telephone (08701) 553255.

Rooms Family rooms and dormitories available.

Prices Over 18-year-olds, £8.25 per night; under-18s, £7.25 per night.

Invermoriston is set in the Glen of Moriston (or Glenmoriston) and you can either turn right on to the A887 which follows the River Moriston back to Torgyle, Loch Cluannie, Loch Loyne, and perhaps go all the way up to the Isle of Skye, or continue on the A82 towards Inchnacardoch Bay and Fort Augustus.

Arriving at Invermoriston you will find the Glenmoriston Arms Hotel on your right-hand side, which is also open as a restaurant and bar to non-residents and offers ample parking space.

Also offering meals is the Glen Rowan Highland Fayre, at the Glen Rowan Highland Estate, Invermoriston; tel (01320) 351352; fax (01320) 351346. Open all year; tearoom and licensed restaurant serving fresh local produce.

The village of Invermoriston has a post office, tel (01320) 351212, and various gift shops, and offers a pleasant walk along the River Moriston as it flows towards Loch Ness, spanned by several bridges, one of which is by Thomas Telford.

One place which is certainly worth a visit is the Clog and Craft Shop, on the A887 road to Skye, where visitors can watch the clogs being made to measure in one of their daily demonstrations. You can also have a browse around the shops and see the quality leatherwear, knitwear, crafts and gifts. Open daily from 9.30 a.m. to 6 p.m.

There are several types of accommodation in the area and although it is situated along the heavy trunk road (A82) it is still one of the quieter spots on the shores of Loch Ness.

BED AND BREAKFAST

BURNSIDE

Dalcataig, Glenmoriston, Inverness-shire IV3 6YG

Tel (01320) 351262

Open April to October

Rooms 1 single, 1 double, 1 twin, 2 rooms en-suite, 1 room private facility.

Prices B&B – single, £17–£18.50; double/twin, £17–£18.50.

Ver Private parking; evening meal available; use of hairdryer.

Non-ver Use of clothes-drying facilities.

Comments Modern bungalow in tranquil woodland setting at the end of country road, one mile from Loch Ness. Easy access to east or west coast. Burnside is situated on the Great Glen cycle route.

STB rating B&B ****

COURT GREEN BED AND BREAKFAST

(Mrs Ulrike Gray),

Invermoriston, Inverness-shire IV3 6YA

Tel (01320) 351287

E-mail courtgreen@ipw.com

Open March to November

Rooms 1 double, 1 twin, 1 family, all rooms en-suite.

Prices B&B – single, £20; double/twin, £18–£19.

Ver TV in room; tea/coffee facilities; non-smoking; private parking; use of hairdryer and iron.

STB rating B&B ****

MRS A.M. GREIG

Norwood, Invermoriston, Inverness-shire IV3 6YE

Tel (01320) 351251
Open March to October
Rooms 1 double, 1 family.
Prices B&B £15–£17.50.
Ver Tea/coffee facilities in room; use of lounge; lounge TV and
    iron; private parking.
STB rating B&B **

MRS I. GREIG
Georgeston, Invermoriston, Inverness-shire IV3 6YA
Tel (01320) 351264
Open All year
Rooms 2 double, 1 twin, 1 room en-suite.
Prices B&B – single, £14–£18; double/twin, £14–£18.
Ver Tea/coffee facilities in room; use of lounge and hairdryer;
    private parking.
STB rating B&B **

MR AND MRS S. LOWE
Burnside Guesthouse, Bhlaraidh, Glenmoriston, Inverness-shire
    IV3 6YH
Tel (01320) 351269
Open February to October
Rooms 2 double, 1 twin.
Prices B&B – single, £16–£17.50; double/twin, £16–£17.50;
    B&B plus evening meal, £24–£25.50.
Ver Tea/coffee facilities in room; non-smoking; private parking;
    use of lounge; lounge TV and iron.

THE OLD POST OFFICE
Invermoriston, Inverness-shire IV3 6YA
Tel (01320) 351322
Open March to October
Rooms 2 double, 1 twin.
Non-ver Vegetarian and special diets by arrangement; use of
    shower, iron and clothes-drying facilities.
STB rating B&B rating

HOTELS

GLENMORISTON ARMS HOTEL

Glenmoriston, Inverness-shire IV3 6YA

Tel (01320) 351206   *Fax* (01320) 351308

E-mail carol@glencass.demon.co.uk

Open February to December

Rooms 5 double, 3 twin, 8 room en-suite.

Prices B&B – single, £42–£55; double/twin, £35–£45; B&B plus
    evening meal, £55–£68.

Ver TV in room; tea/coffee facilities; private parking; telephone in
    room; room service; laundry service; evening meal available;
    use of hairdryer.

Non-ver Packed lunches by arrangement; vegetarian and special
    diets by arrangement; credit/debit cards accepted; use of baby's
    cot; iron and clothes-drying facilities.

STB rating Hotel ****

CARAVAN AND CAMPING PARKS

LOCH NESS CARAVAN AND CAMPING PARK

Invermoriston, Inverness-shire IV3 6YE

Tel (01320) 351207   *Fax* (01320) 351207

Open Easter to late October

Pitches 85 touring pitches, £7–£10 per pitch; 6 caravans, sleep
    12–28, £185–£350 per week.

STB rating ✔✔✔✔✔

SELF-CATERING ACCOMMODATION

GLENMORISTON ESTATES LTD

Estate Office, Bhlaraidh, Glenmoriston, near Inverness IV3 6YA

Tel (01320) 351202   *Fax* (01320) 351209

Open Chalets open March to October; house open all year

Property 1 house, 3 chalets, 2–3 bedrooms, property sleeps 5–7.

Prices £110–£320 per week.

STB rating Self-catering * to **

INVERMORISTON HOLIDAYS

Glenmoriston, Inverness-shire IV3 6YF

Tel (01320) 351254   *Fax* (01320) 351343

Open Mid-March to mid-November

Property 1 cottage, 15 chalets (2–3 bedrooms); sleeps 4–6.

Prices £140–£425 per week.
STB rating Self-catering ** to ***

MRS AND MRS MALIN
Station House, Deppers Bridge, Harbury, Warwickshire
CV33 0ST
Tel (01926) 612928
Open All year
Property 1 house, 6 bedrooms, sleeps 10.
Prices £395–£695 per week.
STB rating Self-catering **

WHITEBRIDGE

TAXIS
MR AND MRS RULE
Tel (01456) 486234 (see page 195)

BED AND BREAKFAST
GLENMOR LODGE
Whitebridge, Gorthleck, Inverness-shire IV1 2YP
Tel (01456) 486697   *Fax* (01456) 486697
Open February to November
Rooms 2 double, 1 twin, 1 room en-suite, 2 rooms private facility.
Prices B&B – double/twin, £15–£18.
STB rating

HOTELS
KNOCKIE LODGE HOTEL
Whitebridge, Inverness-shire IV1 2UP
Tel (01456) 486276   *Fax* (01456) 486389
E-mail 113562.710@compuserv.com
Open May to October
Rooms 2 single, 6 double, 2 twin, 10 rooms en-suite.
Prices B&B – single, £60–£120; double/twin, £50–£80; B&B plus
    evening meal, £85–£115.
Ver Non-smoking; private parking; telephone in room; evening
    meal available; portage; use of hairdryer.
Non-ver Packed lunches available; pets welcome by arrangement;
    vegetarian and special diets available; credit/debit cards
    accepted; use of iron and clothes-drying facilities.
STB rating Hotel ****

WHITEBRIDGE HOTEL
Whitebridge, Stratherrick, Inverness-shire IV1 2UN
Tel (01456) 486226   *Fax* (01456) 486413
E-mail whiteb@worldtraveler.com

Open April to December

Rooms 6 double, 3 twin, 3 family, 10 rooms en-suite.

Prices B&B – single, £30–£33; double/twin, £25–£28; B&B plus evening meal, £40–£43.

Ver TV in room with satellite facility; tea/coffee facilities; private parking; evening meal available; laundry service.

Non-ver Packed lunches available; vegetarian and special diets available; pets welcome by arrangement; use of baby's cot; shower; iron and drying facilities; credit/debit cards accepted.

STB rating Hotel **

SELF-CATERING ACCOMMODATION

STONE HOUSE

Knockie Estate, Whitebridge, Inverness-shire IV1 2UP

Tel (01456) 486648

Open All year

Property 1 house, 3 bedrooms, sleeps 6.

Prices £320–£380 per week.

STB rating Self-catering **

WILDSIDE HIGHLAND LODGES

Whitebridge, Inverness-shire IV2 6UN

Tel (01456) 486373   *Fax* (01456) 486371

E-mail wildside@enterprise.net

Website www.assc.co.uk/wildside/

Open All year

Property 10 chalets, 1–2 bedrooms, sleeps 1–6.

Prices £185–£550 per week.

STB rating Self-catering ***

BUS AND COACH SERVICES

NORTH SHORE
(Abriachan, Brackla, Drumnadrochit and Lewiston, Invermoriston
and Glenmoriston, Fort Augustus)

The bus times tend to change round every six months, though
generally there is about one bus every hour. Citylink travels
between Inverness and Fort Augustus, then continues on to Fort
William and Oban. The Highland Bus & Coach Company
travels between Inverness and Fort Augustus. Both companies
cater for all of the villages mentioned above.

For more details, see timetables at bus stops or contact:

SCOTTISH CITYLINK
Tel (08705) 50 50 50 (lines open 8 a.m. to 8 p.m. seven days a
week; credit/debit card bookings available).
Website www.citylink.co.uk

FARRALINE PARK BUS STATION
Tel (01463) 233371

SOUTH SHORE
(Inverness, Scaniport, Dores, Inverfarigaig, Lower Foyers,
Upper Foyers, Whitebridge)

While there are very few buses which run on this shore, it is a
friendly service and usually on time as there is very little traffic
here. All the villages above are catered for by three different bus
services. Please note: there is no bus service running either way
between Foyers and Fort Augustus. For more details, contact
Farraline Park bus station.